Still More Water into Wine

100 Stories of God's Hand in Life

Helen Brown

Copyright © 2019 by Helen Brown

ISBN:	Softcover	978-0-6485285-0-0

Ebook	978-0-6485285-1-7

All rights reserved. No part of this book may be reproduced or transmitted in any form or by any means, electronic or mechanical, including photocopying recording or by any information storage and retrieval system, without permission in writing form the copyright owner.

Stock images provided by: storyblocks.com

Scriptures taken from the New King James Version ® Copyright © 1982 by Thomas Nelson. Used by permission. All rights reserved.

Cover art by Glenn T Wallace BMM, www.phormulae.com

Production Assistant and Cover design: Wendy Wood

Editor and proofreading: josephineannewrites.com

To order additional copies of this book, contact:
Helen Brown
https://hbrown1956.wixsite.com/helenjeanbrown
or email at: hbrown1956@live.com.au

Contents

1	Being Ready	7
2	Building	9
3	Car	11
4	Celebration	13
5	Chaos	15
6	Decorating	17
7	Disgust	19
8	Egg	21
9	Equal	23
10	Families Remembered	25
11	Favourite Food	27
12	Fix	29
13	Fluffy	31
14	Fog Rolls In	33
15	Four Things	35
16	Fresh	37
17	Fruit	39
18	Garden	41
19	Geometric	43
20	Gift	45
21	Give	47
22	Grey Spaces	49
23	Half	51
24	Hand Drawn	53
25	Hat	55
26	Hello God	57
27	Hiding	59
28	I am Thankful for This	61

29	I Bought This	63
30	I Sat Here	65
31	I Stood Here	67
32	In a Row	69
33	In My Bag	71
34	In My Drawer	73
35	In My Hand	75
36	Joy	77
37	Key	79
38	Leaves	81
39	Local	83
40	Looking Down	85
41	Looking Out	87
42	Looking Up	89
43	Love	91
44	Lunch	93
45	Makes Me Feel Good	95
46	Many	97
47	Matching	99
48	Me Today	101
49	Mess	103
50	Mini	105
51	Moving Slowly	107
52	Musical	109
53	Obedience	111
54	On My Plate	114
55	On the Shelf	116
56	Opposites	118
57	Orange	120
58	Out the Window	122
59	Outing	124
60	Over There	126

61	Overflow	128
62	Part of Me	130
63	Pattern	132
64	Peaceful	134
65	Perfect	136
66	Playground	138
67	Pop	140
68	Prepare	142
69	Private	144
70	Pulled up by the Roots	146
71	Quirky	148
72	Read	150
73	Red, White, Blue	152
74	Remedy	154
75	Repetition	156
76	Reward	158
77	Rise Up	160
78	Rock or Stones	162
79	Sadness	164
80	Small	166
81	Something Far Away	168
82	Something Yellow	170
83	Street	172
84	Surprise	174
85	Teaching Myself	176
86	Technology	178
87	The Blessing of Naughty Children	180
88	The Second Story	182
89	Thick Smoke	184
90	Three Things	186
91	Us	188
92	Walking Out	190

93	Wall	192
94	Warming Up	194
95	Watching	196
96	Weak Spots	198
97	Wet Paint	200
98	Which God is Served?	202
99	Words	204
100	Young	206

1

Being Ready

It was one of those mornings. I was feeling tired and down and I needed some extra sleep. So, after seeing my husband off to work I returned to bed. At about mid-morning, I woke up and tried to decide what to do with the rest of the day. My first instinct was to stay in my pyjamas and do very little.

However, the parable of the ten virgins in Matthew 25:1-13 came to mind. Why would this parable be relevant to me taking the day off? Over the previous couple of busy days, I had let the housework slip a little and therefore not only was the kitchen sink full of dirty dishes, but the bathroom needed some work. The following conversation went on in my head:

"Would you be ready if you had an unexpected visitor?"

"Lord, you know we don't get visitors here"

"But you cannot be sure, can you? It doesn't mean you are not allowed to take time out and rest when you need it but when you have time available it is important to make sure things are in order."

Now I can tell you I don't expect anyone to turn up and surprise me at my front door. However, the conversation carried on:

God said, "It is just like the parable says about my return or your call home, it will be so unexpected. It's not the same as housework but always be prepared for someone to call on you. You just never know when I might send someone."

I did the washing up and cleaned the kitchen and bathrooms, realising that doing these few chores, resting and writing this story helped me to feel better anyway.

No one knows when Jesus will return.

Matthew 24:36 "But of that day and hour knoweth no man, no, not the angels of heaven, but my Father only."

It may not be for a couple of thousand years yet, but we must be ready just in case it is in the next five minutes because God wants us to be ready to meet Him at a moment's notice.

I am confident if Jesus was to return tomorrow I would go home to be with Him.

Will you be ready when Jesus returns?

2

Building

Building bridges is hard work. Bridges are built for different reasons. They may help cars cross over water like the Sydney Harbour Bridge. They may simply make it possible for a train to cross a gully. They come in all manner of sizes, styles, colours and are made from a variety of products.

It reminds me that in every relationship we need to build bridges. We must find a way for different people, from different backgrounds, with different tastes, different plans, and different dreams to find a way to connect.

For us to do this we must put the interests of others first. This is hard work for most of us as we are inclined to put our own interests, tastes, desires and dreams before those of any one else. We can spend years building bridges, working at a relationship then something might happen that brings it all down. We have a choice to either pick up the pieces and put it back together, start again, or walk away.

Each bridge we build will be different because each person we have a relationship with will be unique. Of course, there are some people who will not want to have a relationship with us. It won't matter how much building we do, it will be ignored or discarded. That is their choice and we should not be too stressed about it. The exercise we get trying, will be of some benefit, even if it is only to teach us a lesson.

But there is one person who always desires to build a relationship with us and He is Jesus Christ. He built the bridge on Good Friday many years ago when He died on the Cross for our salvation.

"But God commendeth his love toward us, in that, while we were yet sinners, Christ died for us." Romans 5:8.

He reached out to us first, all we need do is respond to His call.

3

Car

One day while I was visiting my father, I heard a van outside playing a musical tune. It brought back childhood memories of being allowed the occasional special treat of buying an ice cream from a similar van.

I had just been thinking about my grandmother and how when she grew up she had to ride a horse, walk, or use a sulky for transport. My grandmother didn't like horses and told me once she was thankful when the bicycle was invented. She was I'm sure, incredibly pleased when she was able to drive a car.

How far has the technology come in the last hundred years? They are talking about driverless cars! I don't know if I am ready to put my life into the hands of a computer. The news has already been reporting about a car's computer system being hacked, remotely controlled, causing the car to crash.

Again, as I think about how things have changed, even in my lifetime, let alone since my grandmother was born, I still cannot imagine what they would be like one hundred years from now.

But there is one thing I was taught as a child and that is no matter what changes, cars, life, family or even my memories, God is the same today and forever. I can put my life into His hands and know it will always be safe.

Hebrews 13:8 says "Jesus Christ the same yesterday, and today, and for ever." And Lamentations 3:22-23 says "It is of the LORD'S mercies that we are not consumed, because his compassions fail not. They are new every morning: great is thy faithfulness".

These two things I know.

4

Celebration

We celebrate many occasions, but Christmas is a special time of celebration. It's the celebration of the arrival of Jesus on this earth. Usually when we celebrate the birth of a new baby we look forward to watching their world expand as they grow into a toddler, child, teenager and adult. To borrow from a sermon when we celebrate the arrival of Jesus we are celebrating the shrinking of God. God confined himself to a human body, to walk on the earth which had been messed up by sin. He confronted copious temptations, felt sorrow, lost friends, had people spit on Him. People bullied Him, ignored Him, then He was nailed to a cross, died just so we could have eternal life with Him in Heaven.

I agree, the Queen of England wasn't born in June. Yet, here in Australia we celebrate her birthday during that month. Now I realise not every country celebrates the Queen's birthday, but that doesn't change the fact of her existence or the date she was born. I am sure she celebrates quietly at home with her family. Not even my children always get to celebrate their birthday on the actual date.

The arrival of Christ into our world changed many things. When He returns, history will change completely. Some people say because there are no instructions to remember His birth in the same way as the last supper, we should not celebrate Christmas. This would make God a stern, unhappy miserable God. He is a God of Love, Joy and Peace. I think He knew that we would use his birth as a good reason to have a celebration with or without His specific instructions.

Let us celebrate Jesus' arrival into our world in a way that honours Him.

5

Chaos

There are times in our lives when things just don't work the way they should. If I open the hood of my car and look at a modern engine all I can think about is just how chaotic it looks. When I start the car, the engine allows my car to take me to places I want to go. If it breaks down however I would be completely lost if I tried to fix it. Yet, if I take the car to a proper mechanic, they can usually tell me exactly what is wrong and fix it without a great deal of trouble.

When we are children it is our parents who we go to when we have problems. As we get older the people we turn to for help grow in number. However, these people are not always available or know the answers. Sometimes they even give us the wrong advice. This leaves us feeling disappointed. They may not do it intentionally of course but they are human with human limitations.

There is one place we can go to get help all the time. If we go to Jesus, He is always available, and He will always give us the correct answer. He may not give us what we want, but He will give us what we need. He knows, understands how we are made and how we work, better than any mechanic understands a vehicle.

"O LORD, thou hast searched me, and known me. Thou knowest my downsitting and mine uprising, thou understandest my thought afar off. Thou compassest my path and my lying down, and art acquainted withall my ways. For there is not a word in my tongue, but, lo, O LORD, thou knowest it altogether." Psalm 139:1-4.

Do you always go to Jesus for answers to your problems?

6

Decorating

When we as humans are expecting a new arrival, we decorate the nursery, buy new clothes and toys all to welcome a new child into our world. There is often a little more fuss made if the baby is due over the Christmas period. There is something special about the birth of a baby on Christmas Day.

Mary's preparations for Jesus' arrival would have been much the same. New swaddling clothes would have been hand woven. She would have made every effort to make sure they were as fine and as soft as she could make them, so this special child would be comfortable. Toys would have been made from cloth and wood, so Jesus would have something to play with once he was old enough. I wonder if Joseph had prepared a room at his place for the baby. If he had, maybe he felt disappointed that Jesus would not sleep in the room when Caesar's declaration for the population to register in their town of origin, meant he had to leave for Bethlehem just before Mary's due date.

Little did Joseph know as they started out on their long journey that it would be years before they would return to

Nazareth. When they had to flee to Egypt to save their babies life after a couple of years in Bethlehem, Joseph must had wondered if they were ever going to settle down or if they would spend their entire life on the run.

Many of us end up living nomadic lives here on earth. Moving from place to place can make us unsettled because it means we must constantly make new friends. Old friends rarely move with us. We may even be reluctant to make new friends because we know it will only be for a short time.

I know Jesus understands what it is like not to stay in the one place for very long.

"Foxes have holes and birds of the air have nests but the Son of man hath not where to lay his head" Luke 9:58.

Yet, even though He was only going to be here for a short time, He still came and did everything His father asked of Him because of His great love for us. He gives us a job to do while we are here no matter where we find ourselves.

Mark 16:15 "And he said unto them, Go ye into all the world, and preach the gospel to every creature."

Will you make the most of the short time we have on earth to do what God has asked of us?

7

Disturbed

Our dog has this annoying habit of jumping up onto the roof of his kennel. It's annoying because each time he jumps up and down the chain rattles against the tin and makes a dreadful noise. Yet, I must put up with it since the dogs are in the yard outside my bedroom window. As a light sleeper it's a rare occasion when I sleep through the night. On one of those rare nights, I had nightmares all night. I even lost count of how many there were after the first three.

I remember the first three were all the same: someone was playing bowls up and down the verandah outside my bedroom window and each time I went outside to find out who it was there was no one there. They seemed to be trying to break into our home. After the third time, I woke up and stayed awake long enough to realise what I was hearing in my dreams was the dog's chain rattling on the roof of his kennel as he jumped up and down, time and time again. I won't even try to explain the rest of the nightmares here, they were just too disturbing.

What is my lesson here? Maybe, when I take my fears to God my Father. He will show me what they are made of. Is it something genuine, or just a noise trying to distract me from the truth, whatever that might be:

"For God hath not given us the spirit of fear; but of power, and of love, and of a sound mind." 2 Timothy 1:7.

If I remember this, in the future, nightmares will not disturb me for long.

8

Egg

My Easter egg is empty! The cross is empty! The tomb of Jesus is empty! One day all graves will be empty! How can this be? Christ died for me and rose again!

He went through all the pain and agony just so eternal life would be available to anyone who comes to Him and accepts His sacrifice.

As we watch the news we can see many must go through the pain of death, some even on crosses because they are Christians. Yet we know death will not be able to hold them, death is not the end. It is only a doorway to eternal life with Our Lord Jesus in Heaven.

The courage they show during their time of trial is through the power of Christ. His strength is what sees them through and yes when they come to Judgement Day, Jesus will lead them by the hand to the throne of God and say, "Father, these are my friends……, I died for them".

"Therefore, are they before the throne of God, and serve him day and night in his temple: and he that sitteth on the throne shall dwell among them. They shall hunger no

more, neither thirst anymore; neither shall the sun light on them, nor any heat. For the Lamb which is in the midst of the throne shall feed them and shall lead them unto living fountains of waters: and God shall wipe away all tears from their eyes." Revelation 7:15-17.

Yes, Jesus is alive, and He loves each one of us but if we don't accept His grace, when it comes to Judgement Day we will be standing before God with no one to intercede for us.

New life comes through an empty grave.

9

Equal

When I am cooking my "Banana Muffins" I use equal amounts of chocolate chips, sultanas and walnuts among other ingredients. While these ingredients are used in equal amounts, they are not the same and certainly taste different. They all have unique qualities, and each have a different function within the recipe. If I were to leave one of them out, the muffins would not taste as I had expected, but hopefully they would still be edible.

This is what it is like with us as people. We are all ingredients in a recipe God has designed. We are all unique and have a different function, talent, and place in God's plan, but we are all necessary. Some people may be tempted to say, "I'm not important to the plan, no one will miss me if I don't show up, or if I don't carry out my calling." If we remove ourselves from His plan we will be missed. The plan will still be completed but it will be like those muffins ... different. God's plans will not be thwarted.

"For as we have many members in one body, and all members have not the same office: So we, being many, are

one body in Christ, and everyone members one of another. Having then gifts differing according to the grace that is given to us, whether prophecy, let us prophesy according to the proportion of faith;" Romans 12:4-6.

It doesn't matter how large or small the job, or how uncertain we feel about it. We are still an important part of God's plan and because He has the recipe in His hand, He will guide us to fulfil our part.

Let us all get into the mix.

10

Families Remembered

Today, it seems appropriate to remember the other members of the families involved in the war. It was not just the soldiers who suffered. The ones left behind suffered too, even if it was a different kind of suffering, it was still painful. They had to try and come to terms with the fact their loved ones may not return. They were the ones who could not put their arms around their loved ones. How many of them would have given all sorts of things to have such a privilege? Then there were those who cared for the soldiers who did return. Many of them were not recognisable as their bodies were so weak, thin, and scarred from battle, not to mention the emotional damage these men held. It took many months and sometimes years to get these men back to good health.

I'm only guessing here because the family didn't discuss those days often. I do wonder if my grandfather's gratitude to the nurses and doctors who worked so hard during the war gave his work as the local hospital gardener a little more significance. He was a good gardener and the hospital garden wasn't the only garden he tended, but I suspect the hospital one was a just a little bit special.

It took a community to send these men to war and it took the whole country to help them recover. So today I will remember one gardener who came home to recover. He was able to have a family and see his grandchildren, even though I knew him when his frame was to becoming frail.

Age would not worry his mates left behind, they were in no more pain, but I'm sure he remembered them every day.

Let's do the same!

11

Favourite Food

My favourite food is dark chocolate. If I believe some people, it releases the sugar slowly; it is full of anti-oxidants and has positive benefits for my health. Of course, there are others who will tell me there is nothing good about chocolate; it's bad for me. It will make me fat and cause all sorts of health issues. It tastes wonderful and is supposed to help lift my spirits if I am feeling down. Who am I supposed to believe?

In my own experience, it doesn't drastically affect my sugar levels. I know this because I have tested it. I find it rarely makes me feel better when I am feeling down, but I can pretend it will and eat it anyway. As for anti-oxidants, I can't see them and the effects they may have on my body are a mystery to me. If we want to talk about why I am constantly gaining weight and creating all those other health issues, I doubt if I put chocolate on trial, there would be enough reasonable doubt not to convict.

Chocolate still has that "special occasion" feel about it. It's a food we bring out on those occasions when we want to make someone feel adored or there is a special event happening on the calendar. We can even present chocolate to a person to say we are sorry for their circumstances.

Some of this seems a little familiar on another level. Some of us treat God and the church in a similar way. We only go to church at Easter, Christmas time, when someone is getting married, baptized or buried. Sometimes we may even go to church when we are feeling guilty about our behaviour in the hope we will feel better.

God and chocolate have some things in common to me as well. Some people will tell me He is bad for my life and there is nothing out there after I die, but my faith tells me a different story. I find some things are still a mystery and are likely to stay that way. I may not always feel wonderful about my life even with Jesus as part of it, but I know I am better off with Him in it because I have tried and tested His love for me.

Are you willing to give Jesus a try and find out for yourself how much better your life would be with Him in it?

12

Fix

What a lot of things there are in our life that need to be fixed. They range from cupboard doors, bathroom, garden, pot plants and a host of renovation jobs we never seem to get around to. Once we would have ensured we did all these jobs ourselves, but time and age have caught up with us. We are trying to find someone to fix the bathroom.

Besides, the truth is these are all only material goods, they will not last, and they are not important in the light of God's great plan for humanity.

"But lay up for yourselves treasures in heaven, where neither moth nor rust doth corrupt, and where thieves do not break through nor steal:" Matthew 6:20.

I manage to keep the house reasonably clean, we are generally healthy, and the house works. There is plenty of room for all our needs and essentially there is a strong roof over our heads.

In the middle of all these things there is one huge job which is well and truly beyond me to fix and that is me.

The only person in this world who can do this job is Christ and His Holy Spirit.

I have been reading about some of our wonderful preachers in history and one story which struck me was of Robert Murray McCheyne. He prayed it is said "Lord make me as holy as a pardoned sinner can be made". What a wonderful desire to have! Like David I want God to,

"Create in me a clean heart, O God; and renew a right spirit within me." (Psalm 51:10).

Only He can achieve such holiness. It will take the rest of our lives, but with His grace and our determination we will succeed.

13

Fluffy Seeds

We have a great variety of grasses on our farm but there is one which is not useful. It has a fluffy seed head and sheep don't like to eat it, so it is considered a bit of a pest. As I thought about this plant and its seed, I understood why the seed was the way it was. It's made in such a manner to ensure it is light enough to float in the wind and will ensure the grass survives. I thought about the characteristics common to many weeds in the way their seeds are spread. This makes controlling weeds a little difficult and I think it's a pity good grasses and plants have a harder time spreading their seeds around the paddock.

I thought about those other weeds which spread easily, the seeds of discouragement, slander and lies. Once they are in the wind they seem to take on a life of their own. Just like the grass they are not pleasant but spread fast causing sadness and ruining lives. It takes a lot of work to recover from the effects of such infestations, if we ever can.

It takes a lot of self-control or temperance to make sure we are not party to spreading those other sorts of seeds. We need to keep our hearts and eyes on Jesus Christ, so we develop those fruits of the spirit we find in Galatians 5:22-23

"But the fruit of the Spirit is love, joy, peace, longsuffering, gentleness, goodness, faith, meekness, temperance: against such there is no law."

Let's all be diligent in spreading good seeds of encouragement and truth and help lift those who are struggling in life.

14

Fog Rolls In

I woke one morning and as usual looked out the window to see what sort of day we might expect. After a couple of days of rain, the sky seemed to be clearing, a fine day was possible. I could see across the valley to the clouds on the horizon. A few minutes later I took another look and was surprised to see a fog was starting to cover my view.

I was thinking about our future and how there were days when we can clearly see what lies ahead of us then something happens, and the future is again shrouded in mystery.

My thoughts turned to David the shepherd boy. Here was a young man, who knew for certain what his destination was, he was anointed by God to be King of Israel. For a while things seemed to head smoothly in that direction. He could see how things would work out effortlessly even though he knew he had to wait for Saul to be removed. I have a feeling he figured that at some point Saul would die and he would just step up to the throne and take his place without bloodshed and drama.

What happened could not have been further from the truth. Saul's jealousy, fear and guilt meant David had to run for his life and navigate his way through various tricky traps set by the King and his staff. How did David stay focused on the God given vision? It must have felt like the longest fourteen years of his life.

Then I found it! *"David encouraged himself in the Lord his God." 1 Samuel 30:6b.*

So, on those days when we wake up to clear skies then see a fog roll in, we need to remember David, the man who was to be king of Israel, and be encouraged in the Lord our God who has given us a mission which will still be there when the fog burns off.

15

Four Things

As mothers and carers there are four things, we need to make our families feel richly blessed. These would be food, clothes, a place to rest, and a roof over our heads.

The food only needs to be basic and there will be times when supplies are minimal. It may take some imagination to make it stretch a lot further than its limits. We may not have to feed the five thousand like Jesus did as recorded in Matthew 14 but there are many stories being told of how the available food went much further than cooks expected.

Clothes don't have to be of the latest style, but we need to be covered and God often surprises us with gifts of unexpected wearable things. There have been many people who have met this need in others by setting up or donating excess clothes to charities in what we call in Australia "Opportunity Shops". No matter what we wear we need to remember real style comes with confidence in ourselves and our Lord.

Rest is essential, its allows our bodies time to heal and repair. Regardless of whether we are sleeping on the floor or in a palace, God has designed our bodies to recover from the day's troubles and worries during sleep. Besides it gives us the opportunity to get up in the morning and start with a brand-new day.

A roof over our heads allows us to gather our families in one place, a place to care, teach, and develop those important relationships keeping us connected throughout our lives. It may only be a tent, a humble dwelling or some flash mansion, but it is the amount of love and care carried out under the roof that will determine how rich people feel.

God knows we need all these things and He will ensure we have them.

"But my God shall supply all your need according to his riches in glory by Christ Jesus." Philippians 4:19.

Do we remember to thank Him for our provisions?

16

Fresh

What do I like that is fresh? Air, flowers, food, washing, cut grass and water. Each new day is a fresh start as is a new year. Not just on the 1st January each year but there is always the possibility of starting a fresh year on your birthday.

We seem to have an inbuilt need for fresh starts. We read about the greatest fresh start in Genesis chapters one and two. I wonder if the need for fresh starts stems from the way we messed things up way back then.

If you want something to be fresh, there is usually lots of work involved. Fresh vegetables mean a garden must be made, worked, seeds planted, weeds pulled, and water poured on. A fresh flower means weeding, pruning, and watering is a constant job. Fresh washing doesn't happen by magic, even with an automatic washing machine there is much work to be done. Freshly cut grass means a lot of work particularly if it has rained and the grass has managed to grow well before you manage to get the mower out.

But sometimes something fresh is just a surprise. I was mowing this morning and two bright roses caught my eye. The cutting had been put in the ground some three years ago and we assumed it had died. God looked after it and it surprised me this morning. It's a bit like the grace God extends to us; we don't do anything except accept His gift of salvation when He calls us. We then get to have another wonderful fresh start in His strength and love.

"Therefore, if any man be in Christ, he is a new creature: old things are passed away; behold, all things are become new." 2 Corinthians 5:17.

Are you willing to make a fresh start?

17

Fruit

We have a couple of fig trees we inherited when we purchased our property. Over the years they have produced various quantities of fruit, some years very little, other years, nothing has been produced at all.

This year however, despite the drought they have produced a bumper crop. As I collected fruit last night, I became aware not all the fruit was the same. Some figs looked fat and ripe but were in fact half eaten by birds; I just couldn't see the holes from where I was standing and some of the figs were not ripe. Other figs were ripe but once I got them to the kitchen they were destroyed inside by ants and mould. However, some figs were healthy and appropriate to use for cooking.

These trees remind me of the people in our lives. We all live in the same world with its privileges, challenges and problems. Some people are destroyed, others refuse to learn, some look as if they are doing ok but, on the inside, they are a mess, and yes there are some who grow and mature through the challenges life throws at them.

As I think about our fig trees, the first bible story that comes to mind is the one where Jesus curses the fig tree (Mark 11:12-14) because it hadn't produced fruit. I must admit when there hasn't been fruit produced I have wondered if the trees should be removed. They have been left because removing them is a job which is way too big for us, but they look lovely even without much fruit.

Because of the evil in our world, people live through life differently. When life throws challenges at you remember Jesus loves us and is willing to help us produce good fruit.

18

Garden

There was some drastic work carried out on my garden when I was not allowed to do any heavy work. I had to stand by and watch while my husband cut, pruned, pulled, chopped, and sawed those bushes which keep suckering up all over the place. It is the first time the grape vine has seen the sun for many years.

As I surveyed the opened space I couldn't help but think about how sometimes we need to stand aside and watch as God carries out work on the lives of those we love and our own lives. I know I have some bad habits which just seem to keep popping up time and again.

As my husband worked I had to resist the temptation to tell him what to do; otherwise he would have walked away and carried on with his own work. He had been kind enough to put that on hold while he cleaned up this patch of the garden. How often do we try and tell God how to fix someone's life, particularly the lives of those we love? I know I have, far too often then become upset when God ignored my pleading.

Yet, just like my husband, who managed to do a wonderful job in my garden, God does an excellent job with people's lives when we leave it to Him. In fact, He manages to do a great job despite our complaints and grumblings. Look at the way He managed to bring the people of Israel into the Promised Land in Exodus, yet they complained so many times.

Hopefully each time I look at my garden I will remember to give God some space to work.

19

Geometric

If something is geometric, you get a picture of shapes fitting together neatly. They all fit together to make a pattern which can be two or three dimensional.

Many governments wish people were geometric in their shape, size and personality. This would help them because they could treat everyone the same and the people would react the same way. If people were geometric they would do all the same things, need the same things and it would save them lots of money. Some have even tried to build societies around the assumption people are all the same. Their success has been short lived because we are all individuals. Thank goodness God in His infinite wisdom created us all uniquely in His image.

"I will praise thee; for I am fearfully and wonderfully made: marvellous are thy works; and that my soul knoweth right well." Psalm 139:14

We all think, react, learn, and play differently. God made us this way because He wanted us to be special. He knows everything about us. He knows where we fit into His plan, how we fit into the frame of the whole world history.

"For I know the thoughts that I think toward you, saith the LORD, thoughts of peace, and not of evil, to give you an expected end." Jeremiah 29:11

There is no limit to what God can do and He likes to expand our thinking, our lives and our experience of Him, his world and the people around us.

"Hast thou not known? Hast thou not heard, that the everlasting God, the LORD, the Creator of the ends of the earth, fainteth not, neither is weary? There is no searching of his understanding." Isaiah 40:28.

Do you understand just how unique you are to God?

20

Gift

Life is like the gift of soup. When we make soup, we throw into the pot a variety of vegetables, meats and flavours with lots of stock, then cook. I thought about my life's soup when I was praying for a friend who is going through a tough time. As I prayed for her I realised she has been a nice part of the soup in my life even though we have only known each other for a few years.

People who cross our paths leave a mark on our lives, some move on quickly; others stay around for a long time. Yes, all of them add flavour, some we don't enjoy, others we would like to keep adding forever. Yet God has other plans, He tells us not to be greedy, He asks us to share these wonderful people with other people around the world and moves them on to work for Him elsewhere. Our family are the stock of the soup; they are the base we live around, but each day there will be people who God brings into our lives who will only stay for a while. We will always remember their contribution though.

As I prayed for my friend I was thankful for her part in my soup, her positive input and the fellowship we shared. As I was doing this, I prayed I might be like my friend, a good flavour to another person's soup. Please Lord don't let me be a contribution some would rather not keep dealing with.

1 Peter 1:24-25 says: "For all flesh is as grass, and all the glory of man as the flower of grass. The grass withereth, and the flower thereof falleth away: but the word of the lord endures forever. And this is the word which was preached unto you."

People will come and go but what God has taught us through them will have a lasting effect. I often thank the Lord, for my friend, thank Him for bringing her into my life and being with her throughout her life.

Do you thank God for the people He brings into your life?

21

Give

March is a busy month for our family when it comes to birthdays. This means I have a lot of gifts to give. The problem is I never know what the best gift to give is. With everyone now living a long distance away and not seeing them every day I can never be sure of what they need, like or want.

My husband, who still lives at home, is the hardest person to buy for. If he wants something for the farm he goes out and gets it when he needs it. As all his interests revolve around the farm, finding him something for his birthday is a major challenge, not only for me but for the children as well.

I struggle with what is the right gift to buy for so many people and I admit I often put it off. Once my grandson came to stay with me and we went shopping at a plant nursery. While we were looking around his eye caught sight of a small cactus plant and he commented that he liked it. My response was "Oh good, I owe you a birthday present, so I'll buy it for you". His birthday had been weeks before.

As you can see I'm not good at giving. I am always thankful my God and loving Father always knows what is exactly right for me and will always give what is best.

"If ye then, being evil, know how to give good gifts unto your children, how much more shall your Father which is in heaven give good things to them that ask him?" Matthew 7:11.

"Every good gift and every perfect gift is from above, and cometh down from the Father of lights, with whom is no variableness, neither shadow of turning." James 1:17.

No matter what God gives us, it will be the best thing for us, so thank Him for all He sends.

22

Grey Spaces: 1 Corinthians 1:4-9

It was one of those days, when I was in a grey space which happens when you are recovering from a serious illness. It comes when you are well enough to see the things which need to be done, but not well enough to get the jobs done. I was feeling overwhelmed particularly in relation to the amount of gardening needing to be carried out.

All day I was talking to God asking Him for help to get these things done. I debated with all the issues involved. After all I use gardening as part of my exercise routine, but it does mess with my back nearly every time I get stuck into it. I had enjoyed almost three months of a pain free back. On the other side of this debate was the knowledge the state of the garden wasn't that important. It could be left until I was well enough, I reasoned. These and other arguments went on all day, as I tried to do a little bit of work and suffered pain as a result.

God waited patiently for me then asked me about all the difficulties I had been through during my life so far; didn't they strengthen your faith, increase your knowledge and help you to be the strong person you are today? If you do the gardening yourself won't it do the same for your physical health. "Yes", I moaned "but Lord" … His reply was just like the valley of the shadow of death in Psalm 23. This grey zone will not last forever, it has an end and there is a better view on the other side.

Paul was thankful for his fellow Christian brothers and sisters in 1st Corinthians and how they had grown. One day I'm sure I will be thankful for what I am going through, but it is difficult to visualise now.

We need to thank God for the grey spaces in our lives as they are the times when our faith will be strengthened, as we rely on Him more during these times.

23

Half

As I looked at the sky one afternoon, I noticed half of it was covered with black stormy clouds. It was warning things needed to be done quickly. Vehicles needed to be put under cover. Dogs should be feed sooner rather than later. Anything lying around needed to be put away. We could not be prepared for everything which might happen, but we could at least make sure we had done all we could and the rest we'd need to leave in God's hands.

The storm centre was nasty but hit another area. Trees were blown over, some were spilt by lightning, electricity supplies were cut, and many volunteers were called out to help clean up the mess.

There are times in our lives when we can see a storm approaching and we need to prepare ourselves. We will not be able to predict all the outcomes or all the consequences. In fact, I am often surprised just how different things turn out. It doesn't seem to matter how much thought I give to some situations the results are often completely different to what I expected. There are other times when events will just surprise us; there will be no warning at all.

In Matthew chapter 25 Jesus tells us we need to be prepared for one event all the time. This event is our death. No one knows when our time here on earth has run its course.

In the Parable of the Ten Virgins, Jesus tells a story about a party of virgins, perhaps bridesmaids or torchbearers for a procession, chosen to take part in a wedding. Each of the ten virgins is carrying a lamp or torch as they await the coming of the bridegroom, which they expect at some time during the night. Five of the virgins are wise and have brought oil for their lamps. Five are foolish and have only brought their lamps.

At midnight, all the virgins hear the call to come out to meet the bridegroom. Realising their lamps have gone out, the foolish virgins ask the wise ones for oil, but they refuse, saying that there will certainly not be enough for them to share. While the foolish virgins are away trying to get more oil, the bridegroom arrives. The wise virgins then go with him to the celebration. The others arrive too late and are excluded.

This story is there to show us how important it is to be ready to meet Him because there will be no warning.

Are you ready to meet Jesus at a moment's notice?

24

Hand Drawn

My children are not afraid to try new things. I cannot claim credit for having the gene for this trait. One of the things they have all had a go at is archery. Archery is a sport some of my children participate in from time to time just for the fun and challenge of being able to draw the bow. This is measured in pounds. When my son was young he could only draw forty-five pounds but now with increased strength he can draw seventy pounds.

Arrows are powerful weapons which can kill and have been used throughout history for exactly this purpose. They still must be drawn by hand to go anywhere. To quote Charles Spurgeon, *"Arrows, you know, can do nothing until they are shot. The arrow is useless without the bow—and the bow, itself, is useless without the hand and arm of the man who bends it and speeds the arrow to the mark he wants to hit!"*

Spurgeon spoke about arrows of God. "These arrows are spoken of in the plural because while there are arrows of conviction, arrows of justice, arrows of terror, there are also arrows of mercy, arrows of consolation. While there are arrows capable of killing sin, there are also arrows which can kill despair, —and as there are arrows that smite and slay our carnal hopes, so there are others which destroy our sinful fears. And all these arrows are sharp in the heart of the King's enemies—there is not a blunt one in the whole quiver. Notice that all these arrows belong to the King"

God's arm is strong, and it will reach all His loved ones.

25

Hat

There are so many different types of hats for people to wear. There is the hard hat which is supposed to be worn for protection on industrial sites. There is the sun hat, cute cloth hats, which children wear to protect them from the sun. Some hats are just decoration and others can be both decorative and useful.

Each hat is appropriate for different situations and there are some situations where no hat is suitable. As much as I like to wear a hat, I would look silly if I was to wear a hat to the office in this day and age. Sixty or more years ago, it would have been expected, but not today.

How things change! It wasn't so long ago when a woman wouldn't have been seen with a hat on at all but now they are coming back into fashion for certain situations.

When we try to reach the world with the good news of salvation, I think we need to ask God how we are to approach such an undertaking. In the same way we need to pick an appropriate hat for the job we are about to undertake, we need to pick an appropriate approach to spread the word of God.

"For though I be free from all men, yet have I made myself servant unto all, that I might gain the more. And unto the Jews I became as a Jew, that I might gain the Jews; to them that are under the law, as under the law, that I might gain them that are under the law; To them that are without law, as without law, (being not without law to God, but under the law to Christ,) that I might gain them that are without law…………And this I do for the gospel's sake, that I might be partaker thereof with you." 1 Corinthians 9:19-23.

Are you asking God for the right way to talk to others about Him?

26

Hello God

Over the last couple of days, the question of my devotional time has been on my mind. I've never been one to sit down and read my bible at a set time during the day. Most of what I know was taught to me as a child at Sunday School, group bible studies, and through the sermons of faithful parents and ministers in the churches I have worshiped in over the years. Setting aside a daily amount of time for my own personal reading has been met with limited success. I tried it once and found like the disciples *Mark 14:32-42, Matthew 26:36-46 and Luke 22:39-46*, I would just drop off to sleep. I have on occasions used prayer to get myself back to sleep during the night. I have started to pray knowing as the devil doesn't want me to pray, he will make sure I go back to sleep quickly.

Through the posts of other members of the Photo-a-Day group and a message from a friend asking what devotional material I had, I started to wonder if I needed to spend more time doing a "devotional". I was mowing the lawn when this question arose. As I pushed and pulled on the lawn mower, the following thoughts went through my mind. I often do my best thinking while mowing.

"What is a devotional time?"

"It is devoting time to thinking, talking to God about His word."

"When do you do this?"

"While I'm mowing and writing my stories each day!"

The light went on: "Oh wow, I do have devotional time because now I am writing my own devotional each day."

So now I say, "Hello God what would you like to teach me today?"

27

Hiding

One day while babysitting my grandchildren, I found my grandson, hiding behind the door of his bedroom. I had found the silence deafening, which meant it was time to go and find this mischievous little person. When you have small children, silence isn't golden as they say, but usually suspicious.

It reminds me, of how when we are doing something wrong, we'd like to do it in secret. Particularly as children we don't want our parents to find out what we are up to. Even as adults we want to hide it from the public eye. How much easier would it be for the police if all crimes were committed during daylight; where they can be seen and can be arrested straight away. I have been told of some of the naughty things I did as a child, even hiding the evidence.

We are reminded of the reality no matter how hard we try to hide, we are not hidden and cannot hide from God. In Psalm 139: we are told just how much God sees about us. It doesn't matter if we are lying down or walking God can see us. He can even see our thoughts before we speak them.

Verses 11-12 says: 'If I say, "Surely the darkness will hide me, and the light become night around me, even the darkness will not be dark to you; the night will shine like the day, for darkness is as light to you."

I'm sure all of us at some time or other wished God didn't know so much about us. Then there are those days when we want to hide from the world and we find ourselves being grateful He can find us and give us what we need. I'm grateful God always knows where I am and is willing to help me.

How about you?

28

I Am Thankful for This

I could not think of one thing I was thankful for. Even when we were in the middle of the worse drought we have experienced in our lifetime, there are so many things I am thankful for. For the moment I have food, a house to live in, clothes to put on, a functioning computer enabling me to write, and a good number of the other modern trappings of life.

I wake up each morning and as I look out my window I can see the best view in the world. I have a husband and five beautiful children. My father is alive and while my mother is no longer with us I am thankful for all she taught me, the care she gave me and unlike many children I had her in my life for nearly 60 years.

I am thankful I live in Australia, a country where there are no bombs falling daily. Education is available for those who want to avail themselves of it. Employment can still be obtained. Roads are safe to drive on. Entertainment is laid on, and freedom of speech is still possible. Yes, I know these things are slipping away from us but for the moment we still have them.

I am thankful for all my ancestors, those who I have never met. Those people worked hard, battled on through much tougher times than I have experienced, fought in wars, shaped their children and helped make my world what it is today.

The one thing I am most thankful for though is God loved me enough to send Jesus into our world to show me how to live now and after my time is finished here, I will live forever in Heaven with Him. (John 3:16).

How many things can you find to be thankful for?

29

I Bought This

My daughter and I were shopping for some special jewellery to go with an outfit I was to wear to a wedding. We were struggling to find something suitable. Eventually I found a couple of hairbands which were the right colour (gold) and a good weight but they were not made for the job I required. It took the imagination and magic fingers of my daughter to turn two hairbands into a necklace, earrings, bracelet and hair clip. There was even a matching ring available. I have never had such a complete set of the same design before, so I was pleased with the end result.

As I looked at the transformation I thought about what God does with His people. Look at what He did to Moses, (Exodus 3:1-15) someone controlled by fear to a fearless leader. Peter, (Acts 2:14-36) a man who wanted to hide to a man who continually stood up and declared openly of the love Jesus had for all men and women. Then there was Paul, (Acts 9) a murderer who changed and supported those he once tried to kill. They were people who God transformed into instruments He needed to tell the world of His love and care.

I appreciate few of us are called to be the great shining lights these people were but we all have a job God wants us to do. Let us allow God to carry out the transformations in us so we can be effective in the small corners of the world where God has placed us.

How is your transformation going?

30

I Sat Here

I sat here, in bed, and watched the services which were happening over most of the world, those which honoured men like my grandfather, Robert Archibald Deans, who fought hard and long to make sure I would be able to live the way I do today.

I have watched our many leaders give speeches reminding us all of whom these men were, they were brave, strong and courageous. They were regular men, shearers, farmers, clerks, teachers, students, tailors, store attendants, and some were just ordinary boys who hadn't even started out on their life career.

I remember the women who were left behind, their courage isn't mentioned often but it was real. Many of these women were living alone for the first time in their lives. They were taking on the job of being single mums. Many, despite their grief, still got out of bed every morning, fought depression, tears and stress to help raise funds for the war effort and supported each other. They cooked meals for the families with the few resources available due to rationing. They took on jobs which would normally have been done by the men who had left to go overseas.

The Australian men and women of those times dug deep into the strength only God could supply to help them get through those hard and difficult times. Yes, the Christian experience was real to most of these men and women back then. They wanted us to be a great nation where people respected one another, and everyone had a fair go.

Let's honour them, not just for one day a year but every day by respecting all our country men and women and giving them a fair go.

31

I Stood Here

I stood on my back verandah and watched the rains come down. It had been raining all night the first time in a long time. I stood there and praised God for all the blessings the rain would bring.

Thinking about blessings, I'm going to share a poem I heard one day. I have no idea who wrote it, but it goes like this:

Lord, I am Thankful, Lord

For the teenager who is not doing the dishes but watching television,
Because this means she is at home not on the streets.
For the taxes I pay,
Because it means I am employed.
For the mess to clean after a party,
Because it means I have been surrounded by friends.
For the clothes which fit me a little too snug,
Because it means I have enough to eat.
For the shadow watching me work,
Because this means I am in the sunshine.

For the lawn which needs mowing,
windows that need cleaning and gutters needing to be fixed,
Because it means I have a house.
For all the complaining I hear about the government,
Because we have freedom of speech.
For the parking spot I find at the far end of the parking lot,
Because it means I am blessed with transportation.
For the heating bill,
Because it means I am warm.
For the lady behind me in church who sings off key,
Because it means I can hear.
For the pile of laundry and ironing,
Because it means I have clothes to wear.
The weariness and aching muscles at days end,
Because it means I have been capable of working hard.
For the alarm which goes off in the early morning,
Because it means I am alive!

Praise Him today!

32

In a Row

When building a good fence, a farmer will spend a lot of time sighting the posts. This is a long process; the posts at each end of the fence are put in first. Then two people work together to mark out where the posts should be placed. This is to make sure all the posts end up in a straight line, spaced properly and connected with stands of wire so it will do an effective job of keeping the stock where the grazier wants them.

If the fence posts start to move and lean over, those animals wanting to make an escape will be able to do so more easily. These fences are put up with the purpose of making sure the stock can stay safe in the paddocks and have sufficient feed to eat. They enable the grazier to save time when he wants to round up stock for market or treatment.

God continually creates fences for us as well. He works at building fences around us as individuals. His spirit shows us through the bible, preachers and friends, things we need to change in our lives to be better people. He prompts us to learn new things, take on new challenges and inspires us to reach higher goals. All these things are part of the plans He has for each one of us. He doesn't do it in an instant either.

He will take His time making sure all those posts are in the right place, so once they relate to His love and care, we will have strong boundaries and guidelines.

"Commit thy works unto the LORD, and thy thoughts shall be established." Proverbs 16:3.

There will be times when we find it hard to appreciate the fences God has put around us, but they are there for our protection and to enable His work to be carried out effectively.

Do you appreciate what God does for you?

33

In My Bag

I carry a bag with me containing many vitamins and minerals. Over the years I have discovered my body needs extra help to stay healthy. I must admit though I often got slack about how seriously I took this assistance. If I felt well, I would forget to take them until I was diagnosed with diabetes. After weeks of tears and being frustrated with the lack of progress I was gradually put back on these minerals and vitamins to help my health. It was through this professional help, I have been able to enjoy a much better lifestyle for the last eight years. I believe this assistance has saved my life.

No one can save their own life. If we get sick or injured we need the assistance of a doctor, nurse or other medical professional. Even on occasions when I have been able to come up with a solution to a problem without the help of professionals it has still required a great amount of prayer.

In John 14:6 we read "Jesus saith unto him, I am the way, the truth, and the life: no man cometh unto the Father, but by me."

This tells me if I want to live in Heaven after my time here on earth is finished, then I will need the help of Jesus Christ. It will not matter how hard I work; how good I am, or how closely I follow the law of God … without His love and forgiveness I cannot enter heaven.

Have you asked Jesus for His help to get to Heaven?

34

In My Drawer

If you look in one of my kitchen drawers you will find an array of tools which are supposed to help with cooking. They assist in jobs such as peeling vegetables, coring fruits, separating egg yolk and whites, cutting shapes or just holding an egg up right. Without these things cooking is a little bit difficult but not impossible. Some of these tools I see as being useless, but they are still sitting in my drawer. I rarely get them out and put them to use. Sometimes it's because I don't know how they work or I can't be bothered.

I've been thinking about the passage where Moses argues with God about how he is not capable of carrying out the job God has set before him. (Exodus 4:1-17) God keeps telling him He will supply the skills and tools when he needs them. Moses continues to find reasons why he is unable to meet the challenge.

As servants of Christ we have a variety of tools available to us, more now than ever. From time to time I find myself being a lot like Moses. I feel inadequate to meet the challenges of farming life, authorship, and motherhood.

Yet, as I look in the drawer of life I can see He has provided me with tools. They are still in the drawer and I could be guilty of just leaving them there. All we need is faith in God to work for Him. God has provided us with so many tools, but I still seem to be reluctant to grab hold of the power of God and move forward.

In Exodus 4:17 God says to Moses *"And thou shalt take this rod in thine hand, wherewith thou shalt do signs."* I should do the same.

Are you using the tools God has given you?

35

In My Hand

In my hand I cannot hold a lot of things, simply because it's not big enough. Yet, there is a hand that can hold not only the whole of me, but the whole world and the whole of history.

"Who hath measured the waters in the hollow of his hand, and meted out heaven with the span, and comprehended the dust of the earth in a measure, and weighed the mountains in scales, and the hills in a balance?" Isaiah 40:12

No matter what happens we can be sure His hand is large enough, strong enough, and yet gentle enough to care for each one of us. When life is a real struggle I often lie in bed at night and just imagine I am curled up, in the foetal position, in His hand. I picture just how small I am in that great space, even much smaller than Fay Wray looked in the hand of King Kong in the 1933 movie version.

Unlike Fay in the movie, I know there is nothing to fear, it is just a place to rest, be quiet and cry my tears of frustration, sadness, and loneliness for Him to hear.

Oh, what a privilege it is to have a God who cares so much for every one of us. It doesn't matter where we have been, where we have come from, or where we think we are going, He is there, and He will care for us because He made us, knows us, and loves us.

"Behold, I have graven thee upon the palms of my hands; thy walls are continually before me." Isaiah 49:16

Yes, He holds the whole world in His hand, but He holds me gently there as well.

36

Joy

Joy is the middle name of our eldest daughter. I was thinking about her one morning and as I went back in time, I remembered the joy she brought to our lives. The first smile, the joy of seeing her recognise the travelling basket which told her we were going somewhere, was amazing. When she clapped her hands for the first time, walked across the room, these were joyful moments.

It wasn't long though before other memories started to surface. The memories of temper tantrums, fears we might lose her when she was ill, and the stress of watching her lose her way. If I wasn't careful the bad memories would outweigh the good ones.

It reminded me of Pharaoh's dream in Genesis 41 where seven fat cows are eaten by seven poor cows, but the poor cows didn't get fat, they were still poor. The same happens with seven ears of corn. While the interpretation was to warn Pharaoh, Egypt was to experience seven years of famine after seven good years, I find it has an application for me as well. As we go through life it is sometimes easier to hang on to the bad memories which are part of living. If we do our lives will be like those cattle, always poor. It is difficult, but I must hang on to and treasure the good memories in life and this way the bad will not outweigh the good.

I love the verse where after the birth of Jesus, the Bible tells us *"But Mary kept all these things and pondered them in her heart." Luke 2:19.*

She set about remembering the good things, the amazing way God was working, so she would be able to recall them during the tough times.

Do you try to remember the good times in life, so they outweigh the tough times?

37

Key

I was thinking about my mum this morning and how she has gone to Heaven. We know once God's key has opened the gates to Heaven, it is one-way, there is no going back, the gates close tight behind those who enter, and it is an eternal existence.

I was thinking about the fact she wouldn't want to come back to earth. It doesn't matter how much I miss her and how many times I could plead with God to send her back it is not going to happen. As much as she would have liked to be part of our family's physical lives, she is in a better place. Her greatest desire however, would be for us to join her. She would want us to share in her wonderful new reality and save us from the corrupt world we live in. She is waiting for us all!

What is the key to her new reality, the way into Heaven? When Thomas asked this question over two thousand years ago *"Jesus saith unto him, I am the way, the truth, and the life: no man cometh unto the Father, but by me." (John 14:6)* and the answer is still the same today.

"Who died for us, that, whether we wake or sleep, we should live together with him." 1 Thessalonians 5:10

Who died for us? Jesus died so we could have eternal life.

"And that he died for all, that they which live should not henceforth live unto themselves, but unto him which died for them, and rose again." 2 Corinthians 5:15

"For God so loved the world, that he gave his only begotten Son, that whosoever believeth in him should not perish, but have everlasting life." John 3:16.

Do you have the key to Heaven?

38

Leaves

The leaves are falling from the trees as autumn has arrived. They cover the ground creating a carpet of colour. As I watch the carpet grow, I think about us being in our autumn years of life. Our bodies are slowing down; we have passed our prime, even if our brains don't want to admit it.

We have been young and fresh like the leaves of spring, tough and strong like the leaves of summer and now we are beginning to lose our strength just like the leaves of autumn. Like the autumn leaves we still have plenty of life left in us. We can still make our world a better place, share the wisdom we have gained over the years, and contribute to the lives of others.

People react to autumn leaves in different ways. Some people see them as a nuisance, something which causes work and must be cleared away. Some people will see the leaves as great mulch for the garden, a means of improving the soil and helping their gardens grow. Others still, particularly children, will see them as a means of having great fun, piling the leaves into great heaps, jumping into them enjoying the noise they make crunching under their feet.

We will be seen in much the same way, some will see us as a nuisance, others will allow us to enrich their lives, and some will just enjoy us for who we are.

As Ecclesiastes 3 reminds us all, there is a time for everything. Those things will be different depending on our age, circumstances, our place in history, and the plans God has for us.

"For I know the thoughts that I think toward you, saith the LORD, thoughts of peace, and not of evil, to give you an expected end." Jeremiah 29:11.

How do you see those in their autumn years?

39

Local

In many towns you need to be born and breed there to be considered a local. Inverell is a town I consider to be my home even though I haven't always lived there. I consider myself a "local". Why? I have two sets of grandparents who helped develop our town.

These wonderful people where devoted servants of Jesus, serving their church and community all their lives. It is their wonderful example I remember and try to emulate. I cannot do the things they did; some talents have jumped a generation or two. I live in a different time and a different social environment.

What I do have is a faith in God my father, Jesus my saviour, and the Holy Spirit my helper. I have the prayers they said on my behalf and the lessons they taught my father and mother to help me know the truth, love, and kindness which comes from faithfulness.

Those generations who have lived before us seem to be important to God, He listed them in several books of the Old Testament. We need to know where we have come from so we can be aware of some difficulties we might be confronted with as we move through life. If you know a parent has suffered some sort of illness or condition, then you know what to look for in your life and of your children. This won't always apply but it helps. It's another way God will show us and help us to make sensible decisions. He gave us intelligence to use wisely.

"Behold, I send you forth as sheep in the midst of wolves: be ye therefore wise as serpents, and harmless as doves." Matthew 10:16

Do you appreciate the people God sent before you to help in giving your current life?

40

Looking Down

The last thing you would like on a cold winter's day is to look down and see an empty wood box. Without wood our fires go out and we will be cold.

But we all have cold, wet and miserable days. You know the ones when the children are fighting, the husband is tired, and you are feeling unwell. The milk gets spilt, the dog won't stop barking, and the boss makes you feel like a criminal because the report he wanted yesterday still isn't finished. Yes, you know the ones; we all have our own version of them. I'm sure someone along the way will tell you "Look up to Jesus, He will get you through". Well friend, while this is true, I'm going to tell you to look downward as well.

I'm thinking about the Israelites, when they ran out of food. What was it God told them to do? Go out each morning, look down and collect the manner from the ground. (Exodus 16).

I remember reading a story, years ago, about a mother who had a sick child. The mother needed coal for the fire to keep them warm. She went out each day and by looking down was able to collect enough coal pieces to keep her child warm. When the child recovered she went out to see if she could collect some more, but there was not a piece of coal to be found.

Where might we find wood or coal? For each of us it will be found in a different place: our Bible, a visit from a precious friend, the internet, the laughter of a child, or just a few minutes of silence when the dog has stopped barking. God gave us lots of resources to get through any sort of day life might throw at us.

Do you look down as well as up to see God's answers?

41

Looking Out

When the nurse pulled back the curtain in my hospital room one morning, I instinctively looked out to see what the weather looked like. I was surprised to see a heavy fog hiding the world from me.

I had to deal with some difficult situations while I was in hospital. I'm sure you will agree it's always harder to deal with such things when you feel unwell, tired, and weary. My unplanned visit to the hospital while away from home had some other implications, meaning I would not be able to attend a family function I was looking forward to and travel arrangements for my return home were going to create some challenges.

As I keep telling others "life happens" and I must be grateful for the fact I am still alive and there will be other nice family functions to attend. As I hunted through scripture for some insight I read a piece which fitted me to a T. No, at that moment I didn't feel better, but I had those verses to look at and a God to speak to until I could relax enough to be able to accept the situation.

"For I know the plans I have for you," says the Lord. *"They are plans for good and not for disaster, to give you a future and a hope."* Jeremiah 29:11(ESV).

"The Lord is near to the broken hearted and saves the crushed in spirit." Psalm 34:18 (ESV)

As I looked out at the fog on that morning I knew it would clear, and a bright sunny sky would replace it, but I did wonder how long it would take for the fog to clear in my life.

In the meantime, instead of looking out the window, staring into the fog, I must try to look past the fog regardless of what I don't see yet. – I believe this is called faith.

Remember, the fog will not last forever!

42

Looking Up

This morning I woke to find the fire had gone out in the stove. Usually I make sure there is enough wood in it for it to burn all night. Now and again I get caught out and there are not enough hot coals in the bottom to make it go again. This is our source of warmth for the kitchen and family room where we spend a lot of time. I don't like lighting the stove, particularly from scratch. It doesn't always work for me.

So I often cheat on those rare occasions when it goes out. How do I cheat? I gather hot coals out of the heater and carry them on a shovel to the stove. This means walking a considerable distance through the lounge and dining rooms into the kitchen before depositing the coals into the firebox of the stove. During this process I should never look up. It is important for me to keep my eyes on the shovel to make sure the coals stay where they should and don't fall onto the floor.

As Christians we are often told to look up to Jesus, but I believe there are times when we need to keep eyes on the project in hand. To stay focused, to concentrate, to make sure there are no mistakes or disasters. Yes, we need to be aware Jesus is watching and guiding us while we stay focused on the job at hand.

"Wherefore seeing we also are compassed about with so great a cloud of witnesses, let us lay aside every weight, and the sin which doth so easily beset us, and let us run with patience the race that is set before us," Hebrews 12:1.

Let's keep our eyes on the finish line.

43

Love

Many people believe love is all flowers and teddy bears, particularly on Valentine's Day. These were the romantic beliefs I used to have. That was until things went wrong. On a bad day, love didn't feel like love at all. Why did it all feel wrong? There was an instruction which had nothing to do with feelings, well not good ones anyway. It was this:

"But I say unto you, love your enemies, bless them that curse you, do good to them that hate you, and pray for them which despitefully use you, and persecute you;" Matthew 5:44.

They are the sort of people who create bad feelings not pleasant ones. As I worked through this verse I thought about Jesus going to the cross because He loved me and how hard this must have been to do. I realised love was something you do, not a feeling. Jesus loved us, so He went to the cross. If I love my children I feed, wash, teach and look after them.

Feelings are related to romance not love. My smart daughter says, a movie only lasts for two hours. Her point is romance only lasts for a short while, not forever. Love will last because love is something you keep giving by always doing, proving you love your children unconditionally, and yes, your enemy.

"Charity suffereth long and is kind; charity envieth not; charity vaunteth not itself, is not puffed up, Doth not behave itself unseemly, seeketh not her own, is not easily provoked, thinketh no evil; Rejoiceth not in iniquity, but rejoiceth in the truth; Beareth all things, believeth all things, hopeth all things, endureth all things." 1 Corinthians 13:4-7.

Love is not an emotion, is an action.

44

Lunch

Today's lunch was another burnt offering. Last night I had put some extra chops in the oven to give me more room in the frypan and forgot them, until late, too late for them to be tasty. My husband found them this morning and enquired about how it had happened. I told him I would have them for lunch, so they wouldn't be wasted.

As I dished them up, as best I could by adding some pumpkin, I had to ask myself why I was doing this. Was it to punish myself for burning them or was it a case of seeing through the consequences of my actions. Was it even to remind myself not to forget my cooking, something I seemed to be doing a little too often lately? After all we are currently financial enough for me not to need to eat them. There have been times of course, when we weren't as financial, and maybe those burnt chops would have been more enticing. It's not as if the dogs wouldn't have enjoyed them more than I would. So why? Perhaps we just get used to feeling guilty and needing to justify ourselves.

Life, however, is a bit like that lunch. We do things which are not in accordance with the will of God or we move away and there will be consequences. Some of them will leave a bitter taste in our mouths, like my burnt chops, others may not be so bad, but we still must live with them. Yes, God will graciously help us and give us the strength to work our way through them or live with the more permanent ones. What a wonderful gift His unconditional love is.

"Who shall separate us from the love of Christ? shall tribulation, or distress, or persecution, or famine, or nakedness, or peril, or sword?" Romans 8:35.

Let's thank God for the strength to get through the consequences our humanity serves up to us.

45

Makes Me Feel Good

The pain was distressing me. I turned on the light to check on the time ... surely, it's going to be about 5am. No, it's only 2am. "Lord", I prayed, "is this something serious or should I try and go back to sleep". The pain in my neck had been keeping me awake on and off most of the night. I was now trying to work out whether I should go to hospital or not. With the nearest facility twenty minutes away, it is not a decision that is made lightly in the middle of the night.

I was reluctant to wake my husband as he doesn't sleep well these days either. In the end though to stop my fears escalating to fever pitch I decided to wake him. He informed me it was the same sort of pain he had experienced during the last week due to a virus. Once I was reassured it wasn't something serious, I decided to take some painkillers and go back to bed. I felt a little silly and annoyed with myself for waking him during his first good night's sleep in weeks.

However, what made me feel good about this whole thing was at 2 am in the morning my husband was willing to wake up, put his arms around me and comfort me. I thanked God for the kindness of my husband.

1 Thessalonians 5:11 says "Wherefore comfort yourselves together, and edify one another, even as also ye do".

As I thank God for this, I know there are many people out there who are alone and have no one to turn to in the middle of the night. I pray you will find someone to talk to, someone to reach out to and support you. God may surprise you in how He answers prayer, and I'm certain it will make you feel good.

Remember God is always there in the middle of the night.

46

Many

There are so many mobile phone chargers in a drawer we no longer need. The faster technology advances the faster the clutter accumulates. The challenge for me, the proverbial hoarder, is to let go and throw. It's not even a matter of working out if they could be useful in the future. I don't need them, they are obsolete, but I still hang on to them.

But isn't that just like us. So much in our lives is not necessary. It's become obsolete and redundant, but we hang on to these things, sometimes for no other reason than we just don't get around to throwing them away.

We often struggle on in life with extra baggage. If we hang onto it for too long though, we will be prompted by God to lighten our burdens. Once we hand them over to Him we can move forward with a spring in our step. In the Bible we read:

"Cast thy burden upon the LORD, and he shall sustain thee: he shall never suffer the righteous to be moved."

Psalm 55:22 and "Casting all your care upon him; for he careth for you." 1 Peter 5:7.

I have often heard people talk about doing a spring clean. This is a process where the house is cleaned inside out, room by room. All the furniture is moved, the floors, walls, windows and furniture are all scrubbed down before everything is put back in its place. It's not a cleaning process I do in spring; I'd rather be out in the garden then. I do usually get around to doing something like this in the autumn. If I was a perfect housekeeper I would be doing this sort of clean up on a regular basis, just like we should do with our spiritual housekeeping routines.

Have you asked God what you need to throw out lately?

47

Matching

I love things to match. It is something I've always liked. When I was a child we moved a lot of times and as we didn't own our furniture, each move meant a new set of furnishings which didn't accommodate this desire. The décors in these houses were often made up of donated furniture which didn't match. As an adult, finances didn't allow us to buy new matching furniture either. Things still don't match in this house. Why this would be so important to me I'm not sure, maybe it's the subtle influences of advertising during my childhood.

One other desire I had as a child was to match my mother. I often wanted to wear smaller versions of her clothes; you know the ones, mother/daughter outfits. I wanted to be as good, calm and quiet as she was. I am not a carbon copy of her. I knew from a young age I was more like my father than my mother, which was a great source of frustration for me.

What I have learnt though is God made me an individual. I do not match anyone else. Slowly I am learning I am a child of God, unique and like no one else in the world. He loves me because He made me the way I am for a special plan He has put in place just for me, as He has for everyone else in the world. How wonderful is that!

Yes, I know there are still days when I listen to those voices trying to tell me I should be more like my mother or some of the saints of God. I do try to listen to God increasingly but some days the other voices are still a little louder.

"For we are his workmanship, created in Christ Jesus unto good works, which God hath before ordained that we should walk in them." Ephesians 2:10.

Let's all remember God made us just the way He wanted us because we are a part of His special plan.

48

Me Today

As the year is still young, I am, like many of you, standing at the open door. We are looking down the hallway of a new year. What will this year bring is still a question on many minds, as many are not back at work yet.

Many of you will have plans already in place, but like mine last year, they may be changed in an instant. Some of you will know already this year will hold tough challenges. Still others, myself included, will be waiting to see what might unfold.

What I do know about any new year, is each year we live will bring firsts, challenges, and decisions to be made either by forward planning or on the spur of the moment. Those of us who like to be organised or in control will quake when things must be decided in a split second. Some of us worriers will keep going over what we have done, checking and rechecking to make sure we have got it right and those who go with the flow will move on and let the cards fall where they may.

One other thing I do know is this, Jeremiah 29:11 says: *"For I know the thoughts (modern translations say "plans") that I think toward you, saith the LORD, thoughts of peace, and not of evil, to give you an expected end."*

Therefore, no matter what I want this year to hold for me, no matter how many plans I would like to carry out, I need to wait on the Lord God to show me what His plans are because they will be the best for me.

Do you trust God with the plan He has for you?

49

Mess

I'm still thinking about my grandfather at war and it occurs to me one of the most welcomed sights would have been a mess tent. The family understands he was a stretcher bearer and I can only imagine what it was like to hear those words, "The mess tent is over there so go and get a feed". I am under no illusions as to how bad the food would have been. I'm sure the tea would have been weak and not always hot, but it was still better than going hungry. Being wet, cold and tired would have added to the joy of being able to put something into his stomach. However, I'm sure there were days when he would have been too tired or too emotionally affected by what he had seen and experienced, to swallow or chew the tiniest morsel.

These are only some of the trials the men went through to make sure we would be able to live where we are now. Anzac Day is a day we put aside in Australia and New Zealand, to honour these brave soldiers. However, I do wonder what they would think of the mess we have made of the country and economy today.

I wonder if we don't dishonour their sacrifice in the way we treat each other. They were mates who worked together no matter what their previous social status was. Rich, poor, city dweller or bushy were suddenly placed into a position where if they were to survive they had to put all these issues aside and accept what was being dished out to them.

Let's honour our soldiers who cared, worked, and put up with so much more than we ever have by treating all people equally, every day.

50

Mini

I have a new phone! It is, a mini computer. While I can't do all the things possible on my laptop, this new phone is superior to my old one. So now I am on a new learning curve. As I thought about how computers have put most of my generation on a steeper learning curve than our children, I was conscious it probably wasn't nearly as steep a curve as the one Jesus put his disciples on. When Jesus entered the world, He turned all the spiritual ideas and conceptions on their heads.

"Say ye of him, whom the Father hath sanctified, and sent into the world, Thou blasphemest; because I said, I am the Son of God? If I do not the works of my Father, believe me not. But if I do, though ye believe not me, believe the works: that ye may know, and believe, that the Father is in me, and I in him." John 10:36-38.

Just the idea of God being able to communicate with humans in the form of Jesus the Son of God was so foreign to them. They had trouble getting their heads around the idea, let alone accepting it, but accept it many of them did. They walked faithfully with Jesus for the rest of their lives.

When we have trouble grasping a new idea as many of us do, we must remember we are not the first and won't be the last, but God will guide us and help us. All we need do is ask.

"Ask, and it shall be given you; seek, and ye shall find; knock, and it shall be opened unto you:" Matthew 7:7.

Cheers to learning and adapting to new ideas and procedures ... even those itsy-bitsy mini computers.

51

Moving Slowly

Once I heard a story about a minister who went to a church and thought he would like to move the piano to a different spot. When he discussed it with the congregation there was such an uproar he ended up leaving the parish and going somewhere else. A few years later he returned for a visit and discovered the piano had been moved. He asked the current minister how he had managed to achieve such a feat. The minister's reply was he had just moved it one inch at a time and so gradually the piano had ended up in the new position.

As I listened to the story, two things came to mind. This was such a great example of how God changes us. He deals with our sins bit by bit. He cleans us out little by little until one day we are where God wants us to be.

However, the other thought I had was some people think we can make Christians in this way. We expose them to the gospel a little at a time. If they hear it enough and listen often enough, then one day they will be Christians without realising how they got there. Wrong! The only way we can come to Christ is to make a choice. We decide we are going to live for Him and He is going to be our Lord and Saviour. I know some of us, particularly those who grow up in Christian homes, often make the choice but cannot tell you the time, hour or day they made it, only that it has been made. Often God simply whispers us onto the right path.

"Jesus saith unto him, I am the way, the truth, and the life: no man cometh unto the Father, but by me." John 14:6

Have you made a choice to accept Christ and are you watching Jesus change you bit by bit, or is He whispering so quietly that you'll be taken by surprise?

52

Musical

When I was growing up I wanted to learn to play the piano. As my eyes didn't work together properly I had trouble focusing on the written notes and where they were on the stave. This meant I needed to remember the whole of the musical scores rather than read them. I managed to get to about grade five this way.

When I moved to the farm I had another go, thinking as my original eye sight problem had been fixed I would be able to make better progress. However, practice time was limited, with five children and a grandchild to look after, so the dream still wasn't realised.

Would I say this exercise was a waste of time? No, it allowed me some time away from the farm and it gave me opportunity to relate to another woman at least once a week. It was just one of the many things which helped me adjust to my new lifestyle on the farm.

A couple of years ago we needed a pianist to play a couple of hymns for a church ladies function. Without thinking I said I would do it. It took weeks of practice and fortunately they were not complicated pieces. Each time I walked past the piano I sat down and played at least one piece. With encouragement from friends and determination on my part, I was able to give a satisfactory performance.

It seemed like a miracle to me when I didn't lose my place or mess up. Yet I understand God knew someone was required to play that day and I had enough skills to fill the vacancy. I still needed to work hard, and He rewarded me by filling in the gaps.

What a wonderful God we have!

53

Obedience

A combination of my health issues and mum and dad's accident has meant I've become nervous about travelling. It took real effort for me to get into a car and go anywhere, particularly if it was further than to town and back. Likewise, my husband was nervous about travelling on unfamiliar roads.

There was a time when we had a phone call from our daughter. It was important for my husband to attend his granddaughter's formal. It would mean travelling five hours on roads that were busy and unfamiliar. We both prayed hard about this. To help motivate me to get into the car I asked our daughter to see if she could organise a quick book function at short notice. I even tried to arrange something myself. There is nothing like the possibility of selling some books to get me out of my chair. Our son, who is young, confident, and knew the roads better than ourselves offered to see if he could get time off work. The answer turned out to be 'no'. So, we had to plan to do this alone. Yikes! Can't we get out of this! The answer again was no! We had promised, and promises must be kept.

More praying took place in amongst trying to get our nerves to settle.

God we will obey but boy this is putting us out of our comfort zone. Then the blessings started to come in. First, we received a phone call to say things had changed at work and our son was able to have the time off and could help with the driving. Thank you, Lord. This was more doable. However, the book function was a no go.

Have you noticed with each blessing there comes a temptation? Well, the temptation for me was to pull out, just let the husband and son do the trip. God's quiet voice could be heard;

"You said you would go as well"

"But I'm not needed, I could just stay home, I get so nervous."

"You said you would go"

"Yes, I said I would go and I need to be obedient to the promise I made, Ok, I must go." So, I started to pack, and we began our journey still not sure how things would turn out, but I had packed a box of books just in case.

We made our first pit-stop in a town about two hours from home. While we were waiting for our food I was talking to the staff. They asked about how my book was going. When I told them it was slow, they indicated they should buy a copy. They then asked about the best means of getting a copy as their tiny town didn't have a bookshop. I went into my usual discourse of internet sites which carried my book. Then I woke up. I had copies in the car! I could sell a copy right there. They bought one of my books with promises of purchasing more in the future.

We made it safely to the formal and the look on my granddaughter's face while she danced with her grandfather was worth more than any number of book sales.

On the way home, we again stopped at the store where we had sold the book. As a matter of course, I asked if they had started reading my book. Again, God is good, He reinforced my format was appropriate, often busy people don't have time to sit down and read a whole book in one sitting. Bite-sized pieces work so well.

"If ye love me, keep my commandments." John 14:15.

So next time God asks me to go outside my comfort zone, I pray I will remember this trip and obey a little more readily.

54

On My Plate

There was a plate I inherited after my mother died. I'm not sure how she came to have it. It may have been given to her by one of my siblings as an acknowledgment of her wonderful attributes. It may have even been passed down to her from a previous generation. It's not a practical plate, with a decorative gold edge and a verse painted on the base. It would chip easily, get scratched and become unreadable quickly, so it hangs on my wall as a tribute to my mother.

The verse is titled "Mother" and says:

God made many lovely things
Sunsets, flowers, and trees
Birds and starlight, and loyal friends.
And after He made all these
He gave another gift more rare
More loving and more true
A wonderful person most fair
A Mother dear as you.

I am sure all mothers try to aspire to this but for many of us, tiredness, busyness, our own expectations, and those of other people often make us feel like we are never going to make the grade.

There have been many days when if I were to mark my performance as a mother out of ten, I would give myself a two or less. The best advice my mother ever gave me, and I must admit I still have trouble taking it was: "Don't listen to the voices around you". There are many people who would tell us what we should do to be the perfect mother but guess what – they are not living with the people in our lives, our circumstances, our health issues or our personality. In short, they do not know what we have on our life's plate. We are all doing the best we can with what we have. God made us and if we keep looking towards Him, He will get us through

Remember, Jesus knows what is on your plate and He is holding it, so it won't break.

55

On the Shelf

When my father found out about this prompt, he said it should have been "on the table" as in "operating table", as I was to have surgery that day. I had been in hospital a few days before and had looked around my hospital room and there it was - a shelf, high on the wall. There was nothing on it. It was empty. I realised its purpose was to hold vases of flowers given to patients by loved ones.

As I contemplated its empty starkness days later, I thought about all the unseen gifts I would like to put up there. The gifts of gratitude, thankfulness to the staff for their care of me, gratefulness to the kitchen staff for suppling food I could eat, and appreciation for the way the doctors had almost certainly saved my life. These gifts have no tangible form; they can be expressed in words only, written on a card or said out loud.

I am reminded of the person who could be listed as possibly the most grateful person in history, David, the psalmist. How many Psalms do we read where he starts off deep in sadness, depression or weariness, and by the end has found a new thankfulness for what God has done for him? Sometimes he just praised his God from beginning to end.

Psalm 105:1 *"O give thanks unto the LORD; call upon his name: make known his deeds among the people."*

Psalm 106:1 *"Praise ye the LORD. O give thanks unto the LORD; for he is good: for his mercy endureth for ever."*

Psalm 107:1 *"O give thanks unto the LORD, for he is good: for his mercy endureth for ever."*

Yes, the shelf looked empty, but it was filled with the gifts I have mentioned, and they not only filled the shelf but the whole room.

What are you thankful for?

56

Opposites

In Australia, we have great contrasts in our seasons. We have serve droughts and flooding rains. They don't necessarily follow a set pattern. Oh, how much easier a farmers' life would be if they knew for sure a drought would only last two years then would be followed by two years of wet weather. There is, as far as I know, only once where the inhabitants knew how long their good seasons were going to last before they had a drought (well technically a famine) and we can read that story in Genesis 41 and onwards.

In Australia, our farmers must largely work on faith. There are those who insist science will save us, but science cannot make the rain fall or stop. We plant in faith knowing God will send the necessary rain, we put in dams to save His precious gift when He sends it. It doesn't stay there but is used to water the stock until they run dry. God is always good. If He withholds the rain, there is a benefit for the land. When it doesn't rain, there is a hidden process going on under the ground enabling it to bounce back fast when it does rain.

When we face floods in our lives, we soak up the blessings He gives and use them to encourage, bless and serve others? Likewise, when we are facing droughts let us thank our God for the hidden enrichment so when we are flooded with visible blessings again, we will be richer and better able to reach out to others.

"In everything give thanks: for this is the will of God in Christ Jesus concerning you." 1 Thessalonians 5:18.

Whatever comes into our lives, blessings will always follow?

57

Orange

Another internet search found: "Orange relates to 'gut reaction' or our gut instincts, as opposed to the physical reaction of red or the mental reaction of yellow."

It would seem appropriate the fruit called orange is a fruit high in vitamin C which is excellent for healing our bodies or guts.

How much do you trust your gut reaction when you meet someone new? I know my gut reaction to some people is based on bad experiences in the past. For instance, I have met some charming people over the years only to find they are the ones who will be responsible for telling lies and creating unsavoury drama in a situation. So my brain rather than my gut will tell me to be careful. Mind you I have met some people I have been wary of at first and found them to be honest and trustworthy.

In Matthew 10 we read about Jesus sending out His disciples into the world on their first evangelistic campaign. He warns them of the dangers they would face.

He tells them not everyone or everything will be as they appear and tells them to be careful.

"Behold, I send you forth as sheep in the midst of wolves: be ye therefore wise as serpents, and harmless as doves." Verse16. We can be grateful we have the power of the Holy Spirit to assist us when it comes to summing up people if only we ask first and listen hard.

Verse 26 of this chapter says: *"Fear them not therefore: for there is nothing covered, that shall not be revealed; and hid, that shall not be known."*

We can trust God to help us, not by a gut feeling but based on centuries of seeing His work in a sad and corrupt world.

Sometimes, it's better to rely on what our mind and heart tells us instead of our instincts.

58

Out the Window

We have placed a window in our house where once stood a brick alcove holding a stove and open fireplace. This enables me to see the driveway to the top of the rise. This is a good thing as once a visitor's car tops the rise they can be seen, and I can be prepared for their arrival. This is particularly helpful first thing in the morning.

There are of course times when this doesn't work. If I am at the other end of the house I often don't hear or see visitors arrive. We are not used to having many visitors, so we tend to be relaxed about our lifestyle at times. On these occasions I could be easily embarrassed if I am unprepared.

I should remember the parable of the "Ten Virgins" in Matthew 23:1-13. Five of these ladies were smart enough to think ahead and be ready for something that might go wrong. It seems the other five were used to getting by, by the seat of their pants, so to speak.

When the children were young, many people laughed at the number of things I carried around with me either in my bag or the car. This was to try and cover any possible contingency which may have arisen. My bag included the compulsory change of clothes for each child, nappies, wipes, medication, toys and books. We got caught once not being able to have a meal somewhere on a trip home because we had nothing to eat with, so from that day forward the picnic set was always in the car, just in case.

There is one visit which will have no warning. It will be when Jesus returns or calls us home. I have prepared for it, no matter when it comes, as best as I can.

Let's all try to be prepared in our hearts and minds.

59

Outing

If I were to look back down the timeline of my life, I would be able to tell you preparing for an outing has changed a lot. When I was a child I had to prepare according to the instructions of my parents. When we lived in Bingara, we received instructions such as: "You are going to Inverell, make sure you take a jacket" or "Have you had a drink of water and been to the bathroom". As a single young adult, it was often simply a case of making sure I had my keys and wallet and walking out the door. There were no mobile phones in those days.

Then when I got married, we lived halfway between two major towns, so an outing amounted to an early morning trip to town on Saturday morning to get the shopping done before the shops closed at noon, but it was still a case of grabbling the keys, wallet and jumping in the car. Next the children made an appearance and while they were young, getting ready for an outing took on a whole new phase. There were nappies to pack, bottles to make to ensure the children had food, and a whole host of bits and pieces which would enable us to meet whatever unexpected situation might arise. As they grew older it changed again from catering for their every need to trying to make sure they were able to all fit in the car or had somewhere to go if they weren't coming with us.

Now we are a couple again and you might think we can return to just grabbing the wallet and keys. But as we are older it means before we leave (since our memories are not as good as they used to be) we must make sure we have the list of things to do, spectacles, wallets, mobile phone and the keys.

But there is one outing which will not allow me time to check and make sure I have everything …my final outing from this world to the next. God will come and call me, and I must go straight away, leaving everything behind including my broken worn out body.

"In a moment, in the twinkling of an eye, at the last trump: for the trumpet shall sound, and the dead shall be raised incorruptible, and we shall be changed." 1 Corinthians 15:52.

Are you ready to go?

60

Over There

Where is "over there", not here? It will be different for everyone. For instance, when I look out my bedroom window I can see across the valley to the mountains on the other side and I think about the people who live over there. I can often see clouds over there while I experience clear blue skies above me and I think about how their weather is different to mine. I cannot see them, but I know they are there; they have different jobs, different houses, cars, and family situations.

If I look out my front door and turn slightly to my left, I see our shed housing our chooks. While I am not afraid to go over there, I rarely do as my presence upsets the chooks. Maybe they see me as a threat to their quiet, secure life.

I was thinking about how the Israelites stood on the shores of the Red Sea and wondered how they were going to get over to the other side (Exodus 14). God provided a means for them to cross and they moved because they were afraid of what was behind them. I thought about how they stood along the shore of the Jordon River refusing to cross over to the Promised Land and how they refused to move forward because they were afraid of what was in front of them (Numbers 14).

I admire Abram, who, when told by God to go 'over there' where He would show him, he packed up and went. Abram moved into a different way of life and moved forward in faith. As we move forward in faith we will sometimes encounter different weather, things might feel like threats and situations may make us feel uncomfortable and afraid. However, like with Abram God goes with us and all we need to do is hold His hand.

"Have not I commanded thee? Be strong and of a good courage; be not afraid, neither be thou dismayed: for the LORD thy God is with thee whithersoever thou goest." Joshua 1:9.

Let's not worry about what is over there but hold God's hand instead.

61

Overflow

The love God has for all of us is so amazing! His love was so big He allowed Himself to be crucified on a cross, so we could have our sins forgiven and live in Heaven forever.

"For God so loved the world, that he gave his only begotten Son, that whosoever believeth in him should not perish, but have everlasting life." John 3:16

This love flows down through history like a mass of water flowing down a stream after a summer thunder storm. Sometimes, there can be so much water it is unable to be held, breaks its banks, and floods out on to the surrounding fields. Once the water has receded it will leave behind a covering of new rich soil enabling farmers to grow more crops.

The realisation of how precious love is, has inspired some people throughout history to write songs, poems, and dramas, paint pictures, carve sculptures and build magnificent churches and cathedrals. Many of these wonderful creations have endured for many centuries, engrained in the history of our world. These creations were made to honour our God. People often worked hard insisting production be to a high standard to ensure the finished product was as close to perfection as humanly possible.

Of course, not all of us are able to create such remarkable fabrications, however we can ensure those around us hear the gospel by sharing it in whatever way we can. God's Holy Spirit will always be there to guide us, so we don't need to go it alone.

"But ye shall receive power, after that the Holy Ghost is come upon you: and ye shall be witnesses unto me both in Jerusalem, and in all Judaea, and in Samaria, and unto the uttermost part of the earth." Acts 1:8.

No matter how small the job we need to do for the Lord, may we endeavour to complete it to the best of our capabilities.

62

Part of Me

The scars I wear on my body are part of me. The physical scars are a result of some long-forgotten injury. My emotional scars cannot be seen by the naked eye, but they still exist. Unlike the physical wounds which have healed and no longer cause me pain, the emotional ones can still hurt me when a chance remark or action by someone brings back the memories, sadness, anger or frustration I felt at the time.

I believe there are other sorts of scars. They are spiritual scars. These are a result of wounds made by Christians who have treated us badly or preached incorrectly. They can be healed by God but in my experience they take a long time to heal. The devil has so much fun constantly bringing the issues up. He usually has a go when we are tired, sick or feeling low. These are the times he knows we are vulnerable, and the intention is to drive us deeper into the doldrums.

The best way to defend ourselves is to keep our eyes on Jesus.

"Unto thee lift I up mine eyes, O thou that dwellest in the heavens. Behold, as the eyes of servants look unto the hand of their masters, and as the eyes of a maiden unto the hand of her mistress; so our eyes wait upon the LORD our God, until that he have mercy upon us." Psalm 123:1-2.

The other thing we can do is exactly what Jesus did when the devil used Peter to tempt him:

"But he turned, and said unto Peter, get thee behind me, Satan: thou art an offence unto me: for thou savourest not the things that be of God, but those that be of men." Matthew 16:23.

Healing of any kind comes in God's time, let's be patient.

63

Pattern

When you stop to think about it there are so many patterns in our lives. Some are subtle, you barely notice them. For instance, the days get gradually shorter or longer depending on which side of the Vernal or Autumnal Equinox we might be on, we hardly notice. The period of our lives involving raising children might be classed as dramatic and busy and may even drive us crazy, but it is still part of our lives. Other patterns in our lives are big and bold such as the changes in our life stages.

Most of the patterns in our lives will change from time to time. Just like when we buy a new lounge with a different pattern or replace the carpet on the floor. Our time of raising children will come and go as they grow up and leave home. Even our jobs, these days, will most likely change, sometimes giving us a completely different career. Very few of our grandparents had more than one job for their entire working life but their patterns changed when they retired.

Society's patterns have changed as well. When I was born, my father confidently gave me my mother's name because when I grew up I would get married and no one called a married woman by her first name. As far as he could see no one would confuse me with my mother. Now of course, even small children call me by my first name. How things have changed.

Of course, there is one person, who set the important patterns in place and never changes.

"When I consider thy heavens, the work of thy fingers, the moon and the stars, which thou hast ordained;" Psalm 8:3

"Jesus Christ the same yesterday, and today, and for ever." Hebrews 13:8.

I am grateful God's pattern doesn't change.

64

Peaceful

Living on a farm you see a lot of peace and panic side by side. One mob of animals can be peacefully resting under trees, yet in the next paddock they could be running away in panic from a predator. We have spots exuding peace in waves and others where there is always some activity going on. Our lives are similar. One moment, all is right with the world and the next we are trying to deal with some sort of crisis. This is just part of living.

I had been experiencing a week containing more than its fair mix of panic and peace. On one hand I knew God had an answer to my dilemma, but I felt I needed the answer sooner than He was going to give it. I had a deadline (well sort of) and I wanted to solve the problem long before the deadline came into sight.

The confidence I have in God providing the answer doesn't always reach my mind (it is in my heart), but I must admit I had been badgering God for the answer all week. Just like when my children were younger, they would pester me for whatever they wanted.

Psalm 46:10a says: "Be still and know that I am God:"

Yet I still found it hard not to keep asking God for His answer. I knew what the Bible tells me in Isaiah 65:24 *"And it shall come to pass, that before they call, I will answer; and while they are yet speaking, I will hear."*

But still I couldn't wait.

Just as I did with my children, so God has done with me. He made me wait, not because He was being mean but because He wanted me to enjoy the surprise when the answer came.

For some of us learning to wait on the Lord is a lifetime lesson.

65

Perfect

Few things in this world are perfect. When my eldest son was born I thought he was perfect then something happened, and he ended up with a scar as a result. I remember remarking to my mother about how they didn't stay perfect for long.

I know in some cultures certain things are deliberately made with an imperfection in them for the express purpose of reminding us life here on earth is not perfect, we all make mistakes and we should accept life as such.

It doesn't matter what it is we make as human beings there will be faults, imperfections and mistakes. What is important is we do not allow them to be an overwhelming burden. Yes, I know I am just as guilty as the next person. I remember having a discussion with God about how many mistakes I made and how his disciples didn't make such blunders. He was quick to remind me they made mistakes … big mistakes. Once I read through His word, how his disciples were still used by Him to work His plan, those mistakes didn't seem so huge.

Psalm 18:30 says: "As for God, his way is perfect: the word of the LORD is tried: he is a buckler to all those that trust in him."

Even over the last few weeks, things have been less than perfect, but I can see the way God has looked after me. I made certain plans but as He said in Proverbs 16:9

"The heart of man plans his way, but the Lord establishes his steps."

Do you trust God with your mistakes?

66

Playground

Where is a mother's playground? Where does she laugh with her children, learn how they feel, experiment with new ideas running around and round? With them throughout each day, watching while they play ... that's the playground. I know where my mum spent most of her time and where I spent my time doing these things. Yes, the kitchen. At home we had an open kitchen/dining/living area. We would talk around the table. Even when friends came to visit we sat around the table, talked, and drank tea.

As children, we would take our problems to the kitchen, where we could talk it out with mum. It didn't matter once we walked in we were given a chore to do, we wanted to unburden ourselves and mum was the one to listen. Mum was a good listener. Sometimes we surprised her. I saw a certain look on her face many times. She didn't always have an answer either, but most of the time we didn't need her to give us one. We just needed to talk, and we would often come up with the answers ourselves as we voiced our concerns.

It was in the kitchen mum made our butter and learnt how to make bread. These were the 1970's and mum did a lot of these things to make sure we had a better, cleaner and less processed diet and therefore better health. She was a mum some years ahead of her time.

In my kitchen I managed lots of exercise following my children around and round the table. It still is where we laugh, cry and warm ourselves in front of the stove in the winter.

It is where I remember most, the blessing of having a mother like mine.

67

Pop

This was the name the grandchildren on my mum's side of the family called her father. He was Pop. When I knew him, he was already confined to bed most of the time. I don't know if it was a result of his war injuries or just old age. Just after mum's death I was, with the help of a friend, able to find out some more details about him. As I read this again tonight I find some close associations which could be considered interesting.

ROBERT DEANS enlisted in the Australian Infantry Forces during WWI. This took place on 3rd September 1916 at Bathurst, NSW into the 13th Battalion, 23rd Reinforcement. (Mum died on the 4th September 2014) Robert was thirty years of age and a Tailor. He was single, Presbyterian (I do wonder how he became a member of the Salvation Army) and five feet 5 and a half inches tall, weighing 129 pounds. He'd had no Military Service before and his Regimental Number was 7104, his rank being Private.

Robert was wounded in action 11th June 1917 due a gunshot wound to the left chest (my brother's birthday was

11th June 1958) and admitted to 77th Field Ambulance then transferred to Casualty Clearing Station; to 16th General Hospital, Le Treport on 12th June 1917; thence to England 16th June 1917 and admitted to Southern General Hospital, Monyhull, Birmingham on 28th June 1917. On 4th July 1917 he was transferred to 3rd Australian Auxiliary Hospital, Dartford and so discharged to No.2 Command Depot, Weymouth on 23rd July 1917.

Pop died at the age of eighty-three on the 5th June 1970. My daughter's birthday was the 5th June 1985 it means mum outlived her father by one year.

Life is full of interesting associations, but the most important association is our relationship with Jesus.

68

Prepare

Being prepared is not always easy, because we cannot see what the future holds for us. What we require to meet the challenges in front of us is often unknown until we are in the middle of the situation.

Left up to us to be prepared, we would be hopeless at anticipating our needs. What a wonderful thing it is God knows what our future holds and has already provided any necessary skills.

These preparations are often mysterious. In my case, God sent me to get a teaching degree, but it was used to a limited level in the traditional sense. I've asked myself why I needed to go through the hard work and angst. However, upon reflection I see the process taught me much about myself, some of the basic skills I missed out on while I was younger while increasing my confidence.

There will be times when God will expect us to jump in with what we have on hand, just as He did with Moses. He will do this, so others will see His power more clearly. (Exodus 4) We can even argue just like Moses did.

My teaching degree was part of my preparation to enable me to write my daily posts, and the books I have published.

What does God want to do with all this material? I'll have to be prepared to sit back and wait and see what He does, won't I?

"And Moses said unto the people, Fear ye not, stand still, and see the salvation of the LORD, which he will shew to you today:" Exodus 14:13a.

God's preparations for us always come with good reason even if we cannot see the purpose.

69

Private

When you receive a letter marked "Private and Confidential" you know you have no business to open it unless it has your name on it.

Have you ever had someone tell you what you know, feel and have experienced is of no consequence? Well, recently I had such an experience. I felt as if all my life's involvement with God was being totally disregarded. I sat listening to this person and in my head, I was screaming at God saying; "Please tell them you and I have had a relationship and we have been working together longer than they have been alive!"

God's answer was just as clear! "It's none of their business. What I want you to do, who I want you to talk to, and how I want you to work is just between you and me" In other words God was telling me my relationship with Him was our private affair.

I know and believe my relationship with God must be evident to others around me. My life will still have to produce those fruits of the spirit discussed in Galatians chapter 5. This person was making blanket assumptions and I wanted to set them straight. What God was telling me was: "It's not your job. It's my job."

In 1 Corinthians 1:20 it says: *"Where is the wise? where is the scribe? where is the disputer of this world? hath not God made foolish the wisdom of this world?"*

and while some people may accuse me of taking this verse out of context it does remind me if we jump to conclusions about people one day God will show us we are wrong, and we could end up looking foolish.

We may feel as if we have opened a letter, marked "Private and Confidential" without our name on the envelope.

70

Pulled up by the Roots

I was gardening again one morning and as usual looking for inspiration. There was the common theme of plants being smothered in weeds, so weighted down in fact one plant looked as if it was broken. As I started the weeding process I was conscious it was a story I had told many times before. So, I prayed for new insight.

As I continued to weed and tie up plants which had covered my front step and path, managing to pull some plants out by the roots, a couple of things came to mind.

The broken or bent plant would always be a peculiar shape. Similarly, with us human beings, God forgives us our sins, but we are not perfect in a Godly sense. We will be perfect in Heaven but here on earth we will always be a little bent out of shape.

Another thought came to me as I kept pulling plants with weeds. I could throw them away with the weeds, but I asked myself what God would do. He pulls the weeds (sins) out of my life and throws them into the sea of forgetfulness.

"He will turn again, he will have compassion upon us; he will subdue our iniquities; and thou wilt cast all their sins into the depths of the sea." Micah 7:19

Some plants will get pulled out by the roots. What should be done with these pieces? It occurred to me they needed to be planted in another garden bed. I realised this is what happens to us, when we are broken, hurt or disappointed. God uses these spoilt pieces to plant a new garden in the world. To influence others and let them know He loves them, and He wants them to hear His good news. Therefore, He allows us to be uprooted and planted in other places. God can do this without moving us physically; He may bring new people into our lives who have never heard His special message.

However, as I went to plant the new garden I could see there was a great deal of preparation work needing to be done before any planting could begin. So it is with our Lord God, He sends the Holy Spirit before us to prepare.

So for the moment the plants are sitting in a bucket waiting for the right time to plant a new area.

Are you waiting to be planted somewhere new?

71

Quirky

I found this quirky ornament while I was staying with my father. I figured there had to be a story attached to it, so I picked it up and turned it over and around in my hand. The first thing I learnt was it was made by my uncle, my mother's brother, because his name was stamped into the base. The second thing I learnt, just by looking at it. It was a piece of driftwood. My uncle must have picked it up somewhere polished it, varnished it and glued it to the base. This of course is only its short story, the story we all know about. But what about the other story, the hidden story.

This piece of driftwood would not have looked like this when it was first shaped into whatever it was for its second adventure in life, after all its first adventure was growing as a tree.

Was it a part of a ship's hull, a wheel, a bed bunk, a table or even part of the deck? We can only speculate as to what it might have been, it may have been something else completely different, we just don't know. What we do know is at some point in its life, it was thrown into the sea and its transformation began with the force of the sea currents, the salt in the water, the sea creatures playing with it or whatever they do under the sea, and the pounding of the waves. All these things worked their magic and turned it into the masterpiece that stands today in my father's house.

This piece of driftwood is a bit like us, isn't it? We start our lives as unborn souls, we are born, and we face life here on earth. God then uses the elements of this life to shape us, making us something completely different to what we started out to be. Then comes our final chapter, our eternal one. We are picked up by God our Father, polished off and set in place to give glory to Him forever.

How is God shaping you?

72

Read

I read the story of Ruth to my grandchildren. We are studying her in Bible study and I was thinking about my theme on nurturing in the lead up to Mother's Day. What a great example we find in Ruth. She was determined to stay with her mother-in-law, work hard and make sure Naomi was taken care of. I wonder if she promised this to her late husband. We see her faithfulness and determination passed down through the generations and we see those qualities unequivocally in David her great grandson, who was to be King of Israel.

As a faithful daughter-in-law she showed great strength, courage and willpower as she faced the hurdles she came across. She would have continued being faithful throughout her marriage as a wife and mother. God showed His faithfulness in the way He protected both women and lead Ruth to Boaz.

Would I dare say I was as faithful, no way! My mother was like Ruth, determined, caring and faithful to her God. As I faced the first Mother's Day without her, I tried to help and encourage my own children. I am conscious of how many ways I fail to live up to her example. I know I have a different personality to my mother. As mothers, we are often surprised to see how many of our habits and quirky traits are seen in our children. We see them because our children copy us from an early age. I pray each day I will continue to look to Jesus and follow His example.

"Be ye therefore followers (or imitators) of God, as dear children;" Ephesians 5:1.

Let us copy Jesus.

73

Red, White, Blue

I love to do a little bit of shopping when I visit the big city. I don't do it often and I never buy too much. After all, you must be able to get anything you buy home and as we travel by train and bus there is a limit to what you can take with you. Once when I was a teenager I moved from the city to my country town by bus. I cannot remember how many bags and containers I had packed for the trip. I remember my father being amazed at the number of bags coming out of the storage compartment. In those days there was no limit on what you could take with you.

Let me go back to my recent trip to Sydney. I managed to buy a new handbag and a carry-on for the train. While we were looking around for what might be suitable I saw so many colours, patterns and sizes it could have made my head spin. I eventually settled on a blue bag with bright red and white flowers emblazoned on the side. The words "made in Australia" appeared along the bottom edge.

The blue reminds me of the deep blue Australian sky, a sky God put in place with a word.

"And God said, 'Let there be a vault between the waters to separate water from water.' So, God made the vault and separated the water under the vault from the water above it. And it was so. God called the vault 'sky.' And there was evening, and there was morning—the second day." Genesis 1:6-8.

The white reminds me of the purity of His handiwork, there are several times when God looks at His creation and sees it was good.

Of course, the red will always remind me of the blood He shed for me and His church on the cross.

"Take heed therefore unto yourselves, and to all the flock, over which the Holy Ghost hath made you overseers, to feed the church of God, which he hath purchased with his own blood." Acts 20:28.

How delightful many of the colours God created, remind me of His beautiful Heart.

74

Remedy

When I can, I like to use God's natural remedies for my aliments. Sometimes this is not possible; sometimes I must depend on God's inspired man-made remedies for my allergies.

We live in an unhealthy world. There are stresses and strains, illness and pain, death and destruction, sadness and depression around us all the time. Listening to the news is almost a battle of the will not to get depressed yourself. There is only one remedy for these ailments, coming to Christ for His forgiveness, strength, and power.

As I thought about this I was picturing how many of us go to church on Sunday and leave our burdens at the door. We go in, enjoy fellowship and communion with God for one hour maybe more then as we leave we pick up our burdens again. We struggle on for another week repeating the same exercise the next Sunday. The opening prayer of many services often starts with "Lord, help us to leave our worries and burdens aside and worship you."

What we should be doing is walking through the open doors of our churches carrying our burdens inside. When we start to worship Him, we should ask Him to lift them from us.

He says in Matthew 11:28 *"Come unto me, all ye that labour and are heavy laden, and I will give you rest"*.

When we leave we should be leaving with Jesus not our burdens. Then as we work, play, and struggle through our week we will have Jesus and the Spirit of God there beside us to help us. Yes, God has given us knowledge and health to work things out for ourselves, but He still wants to help us.

Will you let Jesus lift your burdens from your shoulders?

75

Repetition

As I think about the different stories I have been writing, I am becoming aware I am repeating myself often. Should I apologise? Maybe. However, as I look around my house I see the same pattern repeated. The boards lining the walls are repeated on top of each other. In this way we were able to build something strong and useful. If we hadn't repeated this process the house would have ended up being weak and useless.

You don't have to read your Bible for long to discover the same message is given time and time again. The Old Testament tells us about how many times God's chosen people drifted away from being faithful and what the consequences were. The message is still the same. God was moving history forward to save His people from their sins. The New Testament repeats we are now living under Grace not the Law and one day Jesus will return to gather all His people to Himself. It reminds us repeatedly we all have a limited time to accept the gift of love taken to the cross by Jesus. This act of love was carried out to extend to all of mankind a way to be saved from their unfaithfulness.

The law says: *"And thou shalt love the LORD thy God with all thine heart, and with all thy soul, and with all thy might." Deuteronomy 6:5*

But grace says: *"For God so loved the world, that he gave his only begotten Son, that whosoever believeth in him should not perish, but have everlasting life." John 3:16.*

Do you live under law or grace?

76

Reward

We all like to be rewarded for our hard work. My husband was recently rewarded with a small harvest because of his hard work in the garden.

The bible tells us in 2 Thessalonians 3:10 *"For even when we were with you, this we commanded you, that if any would not work, neither should he eat."*

I understand there are people in society who are unable to work and need to be cared for, but there are many who could do something, but choose to do absolutely nothing.

It's not long ago when there was no such thing as government welfare. If you needed help, it would have come from members of your family or friends. During our period of prosperity many of these caring challenges were taken over and funded by government departments. This left the general population free to get on with their lives, meaning we worked harder paying taxes to fund these projects.

It has occurred to me recently our society is about to come full circle. Many governments are finding due to the increased needs in our society, they do not have the funds to continue many social service programs. I think this will mean we will see neighbour helping neighbour, friend helping friend, rich helping poor, and children helping parents again.

This is not to take credit away from all those people who do a great deal of work at present. Hopefully when this happens it will mean people will connect with people more, face to face, and I suspect many problems will in effect resolve themselves.

What a wonderful reward this would be!

77

Rise up

One day I got thinking about one of my children's bus drivers. He had a policy of expecting the best of the children on the bus and they usually lived up to his expectations. As I thought about this man and the care he took of my children I thought about how he probably could teach the leaders of the world a thing or two.

He expected the best of the children. I know some of them played up but generally they behaved. They weren't angels, they were children with a child's perspective on life. If we expect the best of people, we must tell them what we expect. The children knew what he wanted, and he allowed them to be children. He didn't force them into a behaviour pattern.

Our society has become accustomed to expecting people to behave badly, so many feel it's ok to live up to those expectations. Rules are put in place to prevent such behaviour; however, these rules are often seen as a mere challenge. There will always be those who will misbehave even as adults, but as expectations have been lowered many people have no idea there is a better way to live.

"Finally, brethren, whatsoever things are true, whatsoever things are honest, whatsoever things are just, whatsoever things are pure, whatsoever things are lovely, whatsoever things are of good report; if there be any virtue, and if there be any praise, think on these things." Philippians 4:8.

Let's rise to greater expectations and build our society

78

Rocks or Stones

As I was talking to some fellow Christians one day, they were telling me about a nice walk along the beach. As they looked around they saw a rock. It was rough with sharp jagged edges but was solid and beautiful. God had made it for a purpose. Further along the beach there were some round smooth stones the same colour as the rock.

How did the stones become smooth and round? The wind, sea and sand worked on the rock, shaving small pieces of the rock off. The water carried them away out to sea rolling them around, backwards and forwards to the shore repeatedly amongst other pieces of rock. As the smaller pieces rubbed and rolled together in the sea, the sharp edges were knocked off. The rocks were buffered around until they were smooth. This process took a long time, years of being moved around and tumbled about in the turbulence created by numerous storms.

I thought about how many people avoid going to church, they find the people are too hard to get along with, they don't feel comfortable, or the message isn't to their liking. Plenty of excuses are used. They will tell you they do not have to attend church to be a Christian or to have fellowship with God. While this is true, spending time with other Christians helps us to grow in Christ. How does it help us grow? It is the process of having to get along with people, relying on God to help us understand the other person's point of view. Putting others needs first despite how we feel and listening to the lessons God wants us to hear. Changing us from sharp rough rocks to smooth round stones.

I used to tell my children God put us into a family to teach us to get along with people we don't always like. This can be true when it comes to our church families as well. We do not like everyone in our church family, and not everyone will like us. However, each time we hold our tongue, don't retort back, pray for someone who has hurt us, we become a nicer person. We become a little smoother. God has told us to love all the people He brings into our lives.

"But I say unto you, Love your enemies, bless them that curse you, do good to them that hate you, and pray for them which despitefully use you, and persecute you;" Matthew 5:44.

It is a difficult process, but it will make us better people for Christ and bring us closer to Him.

"Not forsaking the assembling of ourselves together, as the manner of some is; but exhorting one another: and so much the more, as ye see the day approaching." Hebrews 10:25.

Are you willing to let God turn you into a smooth stone by continuing to go to church each week?

79

Sadness

I walked outside to take a photo of my rose garden. As I glanced at it I realised it was looking a bit sad. There were lots of weeds and rubbish which screamed my absence for some time. However, if I didn't look at the weeds and looked a little higher up I found there were plenty of roses, however they were a little tarnished as we had a couple of heavy frosts during the previous week. It seemed my rose bushes had forgotten they are not meant to flower during winter.

As I walked back into the house (without doing any weeding), I thought about how that garden can sometimes be like my life. I tend to look at all the rubbish around me, the bad news stories on the TV, children doing things I don't approve of, dirty dishes or things other members have not put away. Yes, they do get me down, a lot, but as I climbed the stairs and took one last look at the roses, I reminded myself to look higher than the rubbish. When the children leave things lying around, I can thank God that I have children, many people don't. My dirty dishes mean we have food but there are many hungry people in this world.

I remembered that I must look to Jesus. *"Every good gift and every perfect gift is from above, and cometh down from the Father of lights, with whom is no variableness, neither shadow of turning."* James 1:17.

Why am I so blessed by God's grace? For this there is no simple answer other than He loves me, but wouldn't it be a shame not to share it with others?

80

Small

Small things seem insignificant when we look at them considering the big picture. However, close up we see more details. I took a photo of a small turtle sitting on the pool table. It appeared miniscule and could have been a piece of dirt but taken up close you could see it was a turtle.

How does this apply to us as a human race? The small things we do may seem to be trivial to us, but to someone else they may make a huge difference. It doesn't matter if what we do is a good or a bad thing it may have a big impact on someone's life. A cross word may not be much to us, but it may cut another person down. A smile may not seem much to us, but it may even save someone's life. I read somewhere a person changed their mind about committing suicide because a passer-by had looked them in the eye and smiled.

In Matthew 25:31-40 we read about what will happen at our judgement day. Jesus commends the righteous and condemns the unrighteous people for all the good things they did or didn't do to Him. They are surprised what they did or neglected to do during their earthy lives seemed to be so important to our King as in verse forty we read:

"………Verily I say unto you, inasmuch as ye have done it unto one of the least of these my brethren, ye have done it unto me."

The response to the unrighteous is similar.

"Then shall he answer them, saying, Verily I say unto you, Inasmuch, as ye did it not to one of the least of these, ye did it not to me."

What we think is small or unimportant, may not be!

81

Something Far Away

The words of a famous song are going around in my head today.

"There is a green hill far away,
Without a city wall,
Where the dear Lord was crucified,
Who died to save us all"

While the physical events took place in a country far away from me, I know He is always close.

"But will God in very deed dwell with men on the earth? behold, heaven and the heaven of heavens cannot contain thee; how much less this house which I have built!" 2 Chronicles 6:18

I wonder, if sometimes we wish God was something out there far away. We wouldn't have to deal with those difficult questions of life if He was. It would be easier to blame God for things going wrong in our lives and our world if He was a distant entity, watching us from a far.

But.... He isn't, He is right here, right now, helping me cope with my everyday problems, struggles and questions. He is challenging me to get out of bed every morning. He is inspiring me to write and grow. Even when He seems to be far away I know He isn't. He is so close I cannot even touch Him.

God once told Jacob (Genesis 28:16) *"And, behold, I am with thee, and will keep thee in all places whither thou goest, and will bring thee again into this land; for I will not leave thee, until I have done that which I have spoken to thee of. And Jacob awaked out of his sleep, and he said, Surely the LORD is in this place; and I knew it not."* Sometimes when I look back on my life, I can say the same as Jacob.

Can you see when God has been working in your life and thank Him for His wonderful provision?

82

Something Yellow

We have acquired an interesting chair recently. It was a gift from a friend. Our décor is typical 1950's style and the chair fits in perfectly. It will match our décor a little better once I get around to painting it blue rather than leaving it yellow.

The thing about this chair is it is adjustable. In one position it is a chair which can easily be sat on, then making a few quick actions it becomes a step ladder, something this height challenged person often needs.

So, what can this chair show me about life? I think it exhibits our lives will often require us to be flexible and adjustable. There are times when we will need to sit and listen to our children, family and Our Lord.

"Now it came to pass, as they went, that he entered into a certain village: and a certain woman named Martha received him into her house. And she had a sister called Mary, which also sat at Jesus' feet, and heard his word. But Martha was cumbered about much serving, and came to him, and said, Lord, dost thou not care that my sister hath left me to serve alone? Bid her therefore that she help me. And Jesus answered and said unto her, Martha, Martha, thou art careful and troubled about many things:

But one thing is needful: and Mary hath chosen that good part, which shall not be taken away from her." Luke 10:38-42

There are other times though when we need to get up and do things, reach for things that stretch us a little.

"....and let us run with patience the race that is set before us," Hebrews 12:1b

Let's be adaptable.

83

Street

Like most things in this world, streets come in a variety of forms. They have changed a lot over the years. They do however all do the same thing, even if it's not at the same level of comfort. They provide access to a destination.

I have often heard people say they believe all religions lead us to God and therefore to Heaven, they are just a different route to the same destination. However, Jesus said in John 14:6

"Jesus saith unto him, I am the way, the truth, and the life: no man cometh unto the Father, but by me." so what can streets teach me today?

As I looked at the type of streets we use; the mowed access to the dog kennels, the rough tracks around our farm, the better gravelled driveway or the smooth highways I thought about how those roads would feel different to each one of us.

Some people's lives are tough going, they seem to always need to mow the road in front of them, they plough their way through life. Others walk a track full of gutters and pot holes, but they keep going no matter what life throws at them. Yet others, will move forward along in what could be regarded as a reasonably smooth manner, they have their issues, but life is generally good. While others just sail along with seemingly no difficulties with many blessings and service for the Lord.

Now I'm not saying those who seem to travel the great highways do not have problems in their lives. They do, their journey is simply different to those who must mow their way through life.

There is one place where our streets will all be the same – *"And the twelve gates were twelve pearls; every several gate was of one pearl: and the street of the city was pure gold, as it were transparent glass." Revelation 21:21.*

Are you looking forward to a perfect road in Heaven?

84

Surprise

I think our journey in life can be related to a well set out garden. There are different sections with different styles, different purposes and each section is usually reached by going through some sort of gate or entry way. When we walk into a new section we are often surprised at how the garden can be completely different to the previous section. Life can be similar.

We are surprised by how each phase of our lives is completely different. For instance, we are children, teenagers, young adults, parents of young children, parents of teenagers, parents of young adults, children of aging parents, orphans … maybe we become invalids ourselves and aging parents. Each stage has a different feel about it, a different flavour which is added to our lives and each stage is entered at a point in our lives. Once we have moved through the gates of life we cannot turn back, we must move forward to the final gate at the bottom of the garden. The final gate will hold the greatest surprise for all of us.

There are some things in the here and now which should not surprise us though. We live in a fallen world and there are always going to be things going wrong. We cannot see what might be waiting for us on the other side. We will need to open the gate and step through it in faith. Easier said than done, I'm afraid.

Look at the people in the Bible who God asked to walk through different gates and not look back, Abraham, Moses, Saul, David and Paul to name a few.

If He has asked us to move forward in faith, then He will go with us, but we should not be amazed when we are surprised.

"The steps of a good man are ordered by the LORD: and he delighteth in his way." Psalm 37:23.

How often are you surprised by what you find when you walk out in faith?

85

Teaching Myself

There have been countless times during my life when I knew I had to teach myself something new. It could have been something as simple as breaking an old habit or disposing of emotional and spiritual rubbish. It could be something new like writing. The method that works best for me is repetition. It's an old-fashioned strategy. This method of teaching was used in schools when my mother was a girl. Children were taught such things as their times tables and spelling by what is now known as 'rote'. This was achieved by the students saying them repeatedly until they were permanently imprinted in the mind.

While I wouldn't recommend this for every learning experience, it often works. I've found when I begin the learning exercise I must remind myself that I only need do this differently this once. Not forever, just this once. This stops me thinking I am trying to change the habit forever which would feel too hard. It makes the target, once this time, attainable and achievable. If I do this, every time, I eventually end up doing things the new way as a matter of habit.

In the Old Testament the Israelites were instructed to practice the law of God constantly every day and to tell their children about the wonders of God. This was so they would remember who their God was and how wonderful He was and how He wanted them to live.

If I take this principal and ask God to help me to break an old habit one small step at a time, then I am moving forward in faith and that's all He wants me to do.

86

Technology

When I think about modern technology, which involves computer chips and buttons I automatically think about a poem I used to say as a kid. It goes like this – *"There was a little girl who had a little curl right in the middle of her forehead. When she was good she was very, very good but when she was bad she was horrid."* When new technology works, it works very, very well but when it doesn't, no matter what I do it goes wrong.

I must admit I like old stuff. Stuff with few moving parts and can be pulled apart and put back together again. Things just seemed to have been made better back then. I'm old-fashioned and happy to be.

When we moved into our current house we had a high tank, a tank perched up on a stand above the level of your roof. It's filled with water, then gravity works and when you turn on the taps, hey presto, you have water.

Unfortunately, this wonderful high tank has sprung a leak, not a small one but an enormous one. The beauty of the high tank is if there is a black out, no electricity, you still have water. Now we have had to move into a phase of having our water connected to an electric pump. Unfortunately, once the electric pump stops working so does the water flow! Can you imagine being half-way through a shower when the power goes out and having to wait for three hours to finish it because there is no water? That would be a nightmare.

However, here's the irony of the situation, I wouldn't be able to write without modern technology because I cannot spell for the life of me and I always said God made me wait until someone invented "spellcheck" for me to start writing.

1 Thessalonians 5:18 "In everything give thanks: for this is the will of God in Christ Jesus concerning you." comes to mind when I think about technology, old and new it all has its place.

I would still like to be able to replace that high tank.

87

The Blessing of Naughty Children

For many years I despaired at the behaviour of my children. I prayed relentlessly they would do the right thing. I even enlisted the help of others to pray for them. There is nothing wrong with this and recently I've come to realise having your children misbehave in front of you is a real blessing.

A few years ago, two of my children had issues with each other. One child would tell me something and the other would tell me something completely different. Now, I don't always catch on to things straight away, but even I worked out both children could not be right. One night, completely at my wits end I came home and prayed. "Lord I need you to show me the truth here please. I want to know who is telling lies and who is telling me the truth." A verse came to mind,

John 8:32 *"And ye shall know the truth and the truth shall make you free."*

This may seem like an odd verse in this context, but it set me free from the frustrations of trying to work out who was telling lies and allowed me to peacefully pray for these children. Yes, I know I could have prayed for them anyway and I did every day. However, knowing the truth enabled me to put in place necessary boundaries and to encourage both children when they told the truth.

I have heard some parents talk about how good their children are then listened to other members of the community tell how badly they misbehave behind their parents backs. If your child is misbehaving in front of you, count your blessings because you know what to take to the Lord in prayer.

Nothing is more important to your child's spiritual growth than your prayers.

88

The Second Story

The wonderful thing about the world's history is God wrote it before He made it happen. It has its prelude which can be found written in the Bible.

"In the beginning God created the heaven and the earth. And the earth was without form, and void; and darkness was upon the face of the deep. And the Spirit of God moved upon the face of the waters. Genesis 1:1-2 and *"In the beginning was the Word, and the Word was with God, and the Word was God. The same was in the beginning with God." John 1:1-2.*

We are in the middle of this wonderful story right now, it started with Adam and Eve and will only come to its conclusion when Jesus returns.

"Behold, he cometh with clouds; and every eye shall see him, and they also which pierced him: and all kindreds of the earth shall wail because of him. Even so, Amen." Revelation 1:7.

I suppose you could call Judgement Day the world history's epilogue.

"Marvel not at this: for the hour is coming, in the which all that are in the graves shall hear his voice and shall come forth; they that have done good, unto the resurrection of life; and they that have done evil, unto the resurrection of damnation." John 5:28-29.

Then everyone will live a new story, an eternal one, one which will go on forever. This will be our second story. However, this new story will be written for each of us depending on what we do with the gift of salvation Jesus offers us here and now.

"For he saith, I have heard thee in a time accepted, and in the day of salvation have I succoured thee: behold, now is the accepted time; behold, now is the day of salvation."
2 Corinthians 6:2.

How will your second story be written.

89

Thick Smoke

We woke one morning to an atmosphere full of thick smoke. Apparently there had been some early bushfires burning throughout the night. I remarked to a friend we might need breathing apparatuses to help us through the long summer if this morning was any indication of what the air was going to be like for the months ahead. I was trying to make light of the situation but later I realised many people would be having trouble breathing with so much smoke in the air.

Like the bushfire smoke, sin is a part of our world these days. It's everywhere and we cannot help but move around in it, taste it, and breathe it in.

Thinking about how some people would need to protect themselves against the murky air, I then started to think about how Christians need to protect themselves against the sin in our world. How do we do this?

Philippians 4:8 says: "Finally, brethren, whatsoever things are true, whatsoever things are honest, whatsoever things are just, whatsoever things are pure, whatsoever things are lovely, whatsoever things are of good report; if there be any virtue and if there be any praise, think on these things."

Hebrews 12:2 reminds us: *"Looking unto Jesus the author and finisher of our faith who for the joy that as set before him endured the cross, despising the shame and is set down at the right hand of the throne of God. For consider Him that endured such contradiction of sinners against Himself lest ye be wearied and faint in your minds."*

So, protecting ourselves as Christians is a matter of keeping our minds set on higher things and digging deeply in the strength given to us through Jesus Christ.

90

Three Things

Today we celebrate Australia Day. I started to think about the colours in our flag. Those colours were selected many years ago and I asked myself why? Obviously, they were the colours of the British flag from where our constitution originated. However, I wonder if we look at those colours in a different light, we might be able to get a new appreciation of our country.

Red: Yes, there is *danger* in our country. Our climate means we must constantly cope with floods, fire and drought. The native wildlife creates danger as we live with snakes, crocodiles and spiders. The *passion* I see for our country is immense, no matter how often we get knocked down, the people of this country, get up, dust themselves off and move forward. This country was built on *daring*. The aboriginals dared to survive, adapt, and live not only before the outsiders arrived but after as well. Our early explorers dared to climb mountains, walk in deserts, and cross rivers to expand our living space.

White: It is the *freshness* of our young people and those who decide to join us in this country, will see it continue to move forward in a world struggling to cope with the issues of greed and power. Working together as equals will ensure the hope and dreams of each person is realised, and the *goodness* of our hearts will be shared with the rest of the world.

Blue: We have been blessed with reasonable *peace* in our country's short written history. Economic *stability* has been our badge of honour for the rest of the world to see. *Calmness* and *confidence* are part of our makeup. We have taken these four things for granted and we need to remember unless we take care they may cease to exist.

We are part of a great country blessed by our almighty God and if we continue to keep our eyes on Him, He will continue to bless us.

Advance Australia Fair.

91

Us

There are so many versions of "us". There is the "us" when we are children, with our siblings, there is the "us" when we grow older and become a couple. Then there is the "us" which grows as children are added to the family. There is also the "us" in the extended family we are forced to be part of, then there is the "us" we are part of through our social circle and the support network we choose to be a part of.

The "us" in our lives is like the tide of the sea; it comes in, goes out and comes in again. There are many people who will come into our lives, but will leave, then new people come in, filling the space. Some of these people will elect to leave us for reasons only known to them, others will leave through no choice of their own, and sometimes we will choose to walk away from certain people for our own reasons.

Each person who becomes part of our lives will leave their own unique mark, like shoe prints in the mud. Not all the marks will be permanent, some will be, but not all. Each person will teach us something, either through a good experience or a bad one. The lessons we learn may make us stronger, more cautious, nervous, bitter, tougher or kinder, the choice is ours to make.

The bible instructs us to *"Follow peace with all men, and holiness, without which no man shall see the Lord: Looking diligently lest any man fail of the grace of God; lest any root of bitterness springing up trouble you, and thereby many be defiled;" Hebrews 12:14-15.*

Let's celebrate *us,* good and questionably good.

92

Walking Out

The jetty stretched out in front of me, so far out I could not see the end. If I had to walk down there what would I find at the end? All around the sea was calm and beautiful, but I knew there would be days when the sea would be whipped up into mountains of water capable of washing me off, sweeping me away into darkness and possible death.

The jetty stretched out before me just like my life. I cannot stay standing at the beginning; time will not allow. Time is pushing me forward. It's an unseen force. I must go on for as long as the jetty has planks to walk on. There will be an end to this journey, but the duration is unknown to me. As I surveyed the journey I could see there was a railing on one side only. What if I was pushed to the other side? There would be nothing to stop me from falling. I could cling to the rail, but would it keep me safe or just slow me down? Would there be room for me there with all the others on the same journey?

The voice of God says, *"In repentance and rest is your salvation, in quietness and trust is your strength."* - Isaiah 30:15.

Walk on out says my Lord, this is the way I want you to go. Step out with confidence, walk tall with me. With each step there will be things to do, people to talk to, encouragement to give; I will be with you all the way.

"Let not your heart be troubled: ye believe in God, believe also in me." John 14:1.

"Come walk with me" I hear Jesus say.

93

Wall

What's that saying? "The writing is on the wall". As mothers we often groan when we see writing on a wall. As it usually means "Little Johnny" or "Missy" have found some pencils, crayons or permanent markers and managed to create some artwork where there shouldn't be any. It means extra work to remove it and bring the wall back to its pristine condition. Then there is the graffiti often sending a message, not always polite mind you, to the public as they walk the streets or ride the train. This artwork often tells us people were bored, frustrated or destructive. Occasionally though, there is what can only be described as street art showing great talent.

Messages being written on the wall date back to ancient times when King Belshazzar sees a hand write a message on the wall of his palace. (Daniel 5:5-9) It frightened him, and he had to ask Daniel to interpret it.

Daniel tells King Belshazzar *"God hath numbered thy kingdom and finished it...Thou art weighed in the balances and art found wanting...Thy kingdom is divided and given to the Medes and Persians" (Daniel 5:26-28)*

Therefore, when we say the writing is on the wall we usually mean we are predicting the demise of something.

It would be easy as we look at our society today to imagine the "writing is on the wall". There is so much crime, broken promises by those in power, greed and all sorts of unhealthy behaviour, one could despair of ever seeing the return of what we would consider a civilised society.

There is hope! Jesus came to earth, this we celebrate at Christmas time. He grew up amongst us showing us not only how to live, but how to be better people through Him. Instead of writing this on the wall it has been written in the Bible for us to read.

Are you reading the Bible or the writing on the wall?

94

Warming Up

It's a cold and frosty morning and our wonderful heater has gone out. I'm not surprised as the ashes had been building up for a couple of days. As I poke around I can see there are still red-hot coals in amongst the grey cold ash that smothered the flames. As I shovel out the ashes, add paper and kindling, then watch the fire spring back to life I am reminded of how often our lives can be like this.

If we are honest there are times in our walk with the Lord when things clutter our lives leaving us burnt out. Those things are like the ashes in my heater, the fire is still there, it is just smothered by the clutter. To restart our spiritual fire we must allow God, grabbing our shovel and remove the grey rubbish blocking the way.

"For whom the Lord loveth he chasteneth, and scourgeth every son whom he receiveth." Hebrews 12:6.

The grey stuff is not always sin or bad things. It could be the good and honest things in our lives, but they are just taking up too much room in the plan God has for us. After all, those ashes in my heater (once they have cooled down) are going to be useful on my garden and they will do a great deal of good to the soil but in the heater, they are smothering my fire.

Once we have allowed God to clear the ashes showing us what needs to be removed, then we need to add some paper. Adding paper to a spiritual fire is as simple as opening our Bibles and finding time to read His word. Often when we are busy we read our Bibles mindlessly, instead of pondering and perhaps asking "What are you saying to me today, Lord?" and "I'm so grateful for this quiet time with you.".

Positive attitude is like adding paper to the fire. If we add small things such as a thankful attitude or a smile and reconnect with other Christians, then our fire will take off in abundance.

Next come the big pieces of wood, which God puts back into the heater. These are part of His big plan for us. This is where we start to be effective for God, truly on fire, burning, warming, and influencing those around you. We may not see stadiums of people come to Christ, we may never be able to speak to crowds of thousands. We may only influence one person, but God made us for this purpose, and one day He will say,

".... Well done, good and faithful servant; thou hast been faithful over a few things, I will make thee ruler over many things: enter thou into the joy of thy lord." Matthew 25:23.

One last thought, when my heater has created enough hot coals again I will be grabbing my shovel, taking some of them out of the heater and starting the fire in the stove which also went out last night.

Are you smouldering or burning brightly?

95

Watching

Someone once said "I hate to see you go, but I love to watch you leave" when I first read it I thought it was a strange contradiction. As I read it again, I thought about how I felt when my children left home. Yes, I hated to see them go. As they planned to leave I worried about how they would cope, about how I would manage without their physical presence in the house. We dislike the conspicuous empty space once they move out.

Yet I loved watching them strike out on their own. Watching them learn the lessons I had not been able to teach them. Get jobs, have their own families, travel to far flung places. It fills me with so much pride I cannot help but watch on with love in my eyes. The sudden reduction in the workload was also most agreeable.

I'm not even sure this is what the author meant by what they said but I'm happy to put a different spin on it. Would God ever say something like this about His dear children? I'm sure He would hate to see us go to some of the places which cause our lives to be far more difficult than He would want for us. I'm sure when we leave those places and return to Him, He would cheer loudly. No matter where we go there will be lessons for us to learn, which will strengthen us and enable us to relate to others in difficult circumstances. He loves to watch us grow closer to Him and mature in our faith.

As Christians, how can we expect to be able to understand and help those around us if we have never been to the places they are stuck in? After all, isn't that what Jesus did? He came down to earth as a man and walked in our dark and dreary world, so He could solve our problems.

"There hath no temptation taken you, but such as is common to man: but God is faithful, who will not suffer you to be tempted above that ye are able; but will with the temptation also make a way to escape, that ye may be able to bear it." 1 Corinthians 10:13.

If He could use the power of God here, then so can we.

96

Weak Spots

Recently a friend suffered through an unusually brutal storm. Water leaked in through every crack and gap present on one side of the house. Under normal conditions there would be no leaking. However, when the rain is driven by unusually powerful winds, it will reveal every weakness in the wall, no matter how small.

As we travel through life and storms come upon us unexpectedly the weak spots in our own lives are revealed. They don't need to be violent storms, but when things go wrong and the winds of disappointment and discontent blow, we can find ourselves feeling like a helpless child.

It isn't wrong to have feelings of disappointment, sadness or regret. These are valid feelings which need to be acknowledged, however they shouldn't control how we behave even in the private recesses of our homes. Once our weaknesses are revealed in the light of day, we are then able to make mature decisions for the future.

Jesus encountered many more disappointments and discouraging situations than we are ever likely to face.

Paul talks about the difficulty of being mature when he writes to the believers at Philippi and tells them in chapter 3:13-14 *"Brethren, I count not myself to have apprehended: but this one thing I do, forgetting those things which are behind, and reaching forth unto those things which are before, I press toward the mark for the prize of the high calling of God in Christ Jesus."*

It is only as we practice putting our disappointments behind us and learning to look forward to other projects instead of dwelling on the past that we mature.

Practice makes perfect, so they say.

97

Wet Paint

When I see a sign saying something like "Wet Paint" usually the first question I ask myself is: "Is it really wet?". This question is quickly followed by the temptation to touch and find out for myself. It seems I have a genuine distrust of "Wet Paint" signs. I don't seem to be able to take them at their word.

I find myself doing the same thing with the signs God places in front of me. I don't always take him at His word. If I did I would trust Him more often. I can blog, write, chat and talk until the cows come home about how He is faithful, but if I do not trust Him enough to respond to His instructions, then I am wasting my time, energy, and breath.

Numbers 23:29 says "God is not a man, that he should lie; neither the son of man, that he should repent: hath he said, and shall he not do it? or hath he spoken, and shall he not make it good?"

This is a sign God gives us all about who He is and what He can do, and what He will not do. If I believe this sign to be true, I step out and trust Him for all the things in my life.

1 John 1:9 says: *"If we confess our sins, he is faithful and just to forgive us our sins, and to cleanse us from all unrighteousness."*

There is an entire book which holds all the signs that God wants us to take notice of. Will you open it?

Let's read the signs and find out what God wants us to do?

98

Which God is Served?

A photograph was taken of a cityscape; it was taken from an office block window facing a church. When it was built this church would have been, the tallest building in the city, but now it was dwarfed by the other office buildings around it. It seemed small and insignificant. As I looked at the photograph, it seemed to capture the truth of some thoughts I had been dealing with over the past few days. It is a great indicator of the priority of our society today. Previously the church would have been the pivotal part of the city with God and all His grace coming first and foremost in people's lives. Now commercial buildings hide this humble church, which may show us the god we worship today is money and there is no grace extended by this god. It demands we treat people as a liability not the asset they are to any business.

As I read and hear stories of the struggles and hardships of our farmers, refugees and asylum seekers, and many young women here and overseas, I am left heart broken. There is no greater indicator proving the leaders of our country and the world are serving the god of money and not the one true God.

Growing up, I heard stories of how people would starve themselves to provide sacrificial food to be placed in front of the idols of their gods, rather than using it to feed themselves and their hungry children. Such are the demands of false gods. They demand you neglect yourself, your family, neighbours, the poor, the vulnerable, to serve them.

In Matthew 6:19 we are warned: *"Lay not up for yourselves treasures upon earth, where moth and rust doth corrupt, and where thieves break through and steal;"*

Verse 24 tells us *"No man can serve two masters; for either he will hate the one and love the other; or else he will hold to the one and despise the other. Ye cannot serve God and mannon."*

When we serve the one true God we think about **J**esus, **O**thers and **Y**ou in that order.

How much genuine joy do we see in this world of ours today?

99

Words

Sometimes words are just words; they are without meaning. Having missed a recent family wedding, I had to rely on the words of others to know how the event went. Yes, there have been some photos and keepsakes, but it is the descriptions of those who were there which paint the real pictures for me. Photos cannot tell me about the emotional tone of the day, the respect shown to those in the party or the family. It is their words that tell me how tired people are because they have worked so hard to make this event happen, or how happy others were to be there.

One of the most important things about a wedding though, is it marks the beginning of a marriage, a lifetime of living, loving, and caring for each other and the children who may come along later.

"For this cause shall a man leave his father and mother and cleave to his wife; And they twain shall be one flesh: so, then they are no more twain, but one flesh." Mark 10:7-8.

When a couple stand up in front of family and friends and say "I do" making promises to each other, I am sure most of those couples intend to faithfully keep those promises. Sadly, there are occasions when people do stand up and say "I do" without understanding the meaning of their words. This is an occasion where words are just words.

Someone has said they wanted a marriage and not just a wedding. This is when those words of promise have great meaning.

In this case, it doesn't matter how things turn out on the day. The weather may be glorious, or it could be raining a torrent, the venue may be horrid or the food awful, however this couple have begun a new life together, and that's the most important thing.

May my words not be just words, but words of encouragement and love.

100

Young

When we are young, we have dreams. Some of those dreams are too big for anyone but others are achievable. Some dreams don't consider our abilities, social restrictions or other boundaries which may exist when we grow up. Even as parents we often have dreams for our children when they are too young for us to know or understand their likes, dislikes and personalities.

Some people will say if you have a dream it is possible. They'll tell you the only thing stopping you is hard work and your vision. The thing is, there have been some assumptions made here. The first is that your dreams are legal. I have heard of some rather dubious dreams at times. The next one is you will have the talents to do what your dreams require. We are all given talents and it's up to us to use them appropriately. There's no point in hanging onto pipe-dreams. We are all geniuses in our own expertise. Albert Einstein wrote, "Everybody is a genius. But if you judge a fish by its ability to climb a tree, it will live its whole life believing that it is stupid." The question I have for you at this point of our journey together is, "What is your genius?"

Taken from "The Rhythm of Life: Living Every Day with Passion and Purpose" by Matthew Kelly

Recently I heard a hymn I had not heard before and one line stuck in my mind. It went something along of the lines of, *"thank you for the prayers you granted and the ones that you didn't."* So often we think we would like something, we think it will be good for us, but God knows different.

A Songs of Praise programme talked about how three people succumbed to various temptations and how their lives were destroyed. Not all these temptations were bad things in themselves; they were just the wrong things to have controlling their lives.

There is one question about our dreams and aspirations we rarely ask ourselves: "Is this the dream God has for us?" I'm remembering George Muller who wanted to go to China to be a missionary, but God wanted him to go to Bristol to look after children. He did eventually go to China but as I understand, it was not as a missionary.

I Corinthians 2:9 says *"But as it is written, Eye hath not seen, nor ear heard, neither have entered into the heart of man, the things which God hath prepared for them that love him."*

Sometimes we are taken to places we never dreamed of. Are our dreams from God or are we all trying to be a fish climbing a tree?

Other Books available

by this Author

Turning Water into Wine –
100 Stories of God's hand in Life

More Water into Wine –
100 Stories of God's hand in Life

Reflections –
Australian Stories from my Father's Past

365 Glasses of Wine –
Devotionals for each day of the year

Conversations with Myself, Vol 1 –
100 Stories of Hope, Faith and Determination

All these books are available in Paperback & ebook formats from Amazon.com, Barnes & Noble and Xlibris.com
Printed Copies are also available from the Author at
https://hbrown1956.wixsite.com/helenjeanbrown
or email: hbrown1956@live.com.au

www.ingramcontent.com/pod-product-compliance
Lightning Source LLC
Chambersburg PA
CBHW031416290426
44110CB00011B/403